Choose Peace

Presented by
Soka Gakkai International-USA

In commemoration of

Seeds of Change:
The Earth Charter and Human Potential

Exhibited at the
Grace Mellman Community Library
August 3rd-14th, 2010.

Choose Peace

**A Dialogue between
Johan Galtung and Daisaku Ikeda**

Translated and edited by Richard L. Gage

Pluto  Press

LONDON • STERLING, VIRGINIA

First published 1995 by Pluto Press
345 Archway Road, London N6 5AA
and 22883 Quicksilver Drive, Sterling, VA 20166-2012, USA

British Library Cataloguing in Publication Data
A catalogue record for this book is available from the British
Library

ISBN 0 7453 1040 0 hbk
     0 7453 1039 7 pbk

Library of Congress Cataloging in Publication Data
Galtung, Johan.
   Choose peace/a dialogue between Johan Galtung and
Daisaku Ikeda; translated and edited by Richard L. Gage.
      p.   cm.
   ISBN 0–7453–1039–7 (pbk.). — ISBN 0–7453–1040–0 (hb)
   1. Peace—Religious aspects—Buddhism. 2. Buddhism—Social
aspects. I. Ikeda, Daisaku. II. Gage, Richard L. III. Title.
BQ4570.P4G35   1995
294.3'37873—dc20   94–13591
                                                        CIP

10   9   8   7   6   5   4   3

Designed and produced for Pluto Press by
Chase Publishing Services
Typeset from disk by Stanford DTP Services, Towcester
Printed in the European Union by
Antony Rowe, Chippenham and Eastbourne, England

Contents

About the Authors

Johan Galtung

Johan Galtung is one of the founders of modern peace studies. He was born in Oslo in 1930 and, as a child, experienced the German occupation of Norway and his father's imprisonment in a concentration camp for resistance. These events left a lasting impression on him and led him, inspired by Mahatma Gandhi's ideas and political action, to question how World War II – and in particular occupation – could have been prevented and, furthermore, how the occupation of Norway could have been resisted nonviolently. Subsequently, as a conscientious objector to military service, he spent six months in prison in Norway.

In 1959 he founded the first International Peace Research Institute in Oslo, and in 1964 co-founded the International Peace Research Association. The same year he launched the *Journal of Peace Research*. Professor Galtung has taught at over 50 universities around the world and currently holds positions at four of them. His honours include five honorary doctorates and four honorary professorships. For his work on peace studies in higher education he was awarded the Right Livelihood Award (or the 'Alternative Nobel Peace Prize') in 1987. He is also the holder of the Norwegian Humanist Prize, 1987; the Socrates Prize for Adult Education, 1990, and the Bajaj International Award for Promoting Gandhian Values, 1993.

As an activist for peace, Professor Galtung has now worked in and with peace movements for over 35 years and has intervened in many conflicts around the world. Fundamental to his approach to conflict-resolution are the concepts of nonviolence and transcendence, implemented by working with conflict parties, indicating nonviolent ways of attaining goals and overcoming conflict through creative thought, speech and action. Spiritually, Professor Galtung is very much at home in Buddhism, but also considers himself a humanist with an interest in the gentler aspects of all religions.

Professor Galtung has lectured and written widely on peace studies. He has published more than 70 books on peace studies, social studies and social science methodology, including *Peace: Research, Education Action* (Copenhagen: Ejliers 1975) and, more recently, *Human Rights in Another Key* (Cambridge: Cambridge University Press 1994) and *Peace by Peaceful Means* (London: Sage 1995).

Daisaku Ikeda

Daisaku Ikeda is a leading Buddhist, author and educator who firmly holds that dialogue is the key to surmounting cultural and philosophical boundaries and forging the mutual trust and understanding necessary for lasting peace.

Born in 1928 in Tokyo, Daisaku Ikeda's awareness of the need to struggle for peace began at an early age. The torment of World War II, and particularly the death of his eldest brother in combat, and the anguish of postwar Japan, left an indelible impression on him and has fueled his lifelong efforts to root out the fundamental causes of human conflict. He joined Soka Gakkai – a Buddhist lay organization – in 1943, soon after meeting Josei Toda (1900–1958), the man who was to become his mentor. Toda was imprisoned in 1943 along with Tsunesaburo Makiguchi, the first president of Soka Gakkai, for opposing Japanese militarism. Both men were innovative educators and, under Toda's tutelage, Daisaku Ikeda continued his education in philosophy, literature, physical and life sciences, economics, politics and other disciplines. For more than a decade Toda and Ikeda shaped and developed Soka Gakkai's movement for peace, culture and education. In 1960, two years after Josei Toda's death, Ikeda became president of Soka Gakkai, and in 1975 he became president of Soka Gakkai International (SGI), which now has members in 115 countries.

Daisaku Ikeda defines the objectives of the SGI as 'contributing to peace and the welfare of humankind by promoting humanitarian culture and education and opposing all forms of violence'. He views peace not merely as the absence of war, but as a condition in which the dignity and fundamental rights of all people are respected. To achieve this goal, Ikeda emphasizes the importance of working with the United Nations. Accordingly, he has addressed numerous proposals on peace and international affairs to the UN. Ikeda approaches global problems with the conviction that an age of hope, humanism and coexistence is achievable. His belief that peace must come from within is based on the Buddhist view that all individuals inherently possess the ability to create value in society and achieve harmony between themselves and their environment. Culture, he holds, is the lively expression of this uniquely human potential, while education is an essential vehicle for its development.

Daisaku Ikeda has founded several institutions, including the Soka schools, the Min-On Concert Association and the Tokyo Fuji Art Museum. He has also initiated a wide range of grassroots exchange programmes and delivered speeches at a number of institutions of higher learning around the world, including Harvard University, the Institut de France and Beijing University.

Preface

We first met in December 1984, on the occasion of a conference on the subject of 'Buddhism and Leadership for Peace', organized by the Peace Research Institute of Soka University in Tokyo. Our mutual friend Professor Glenn D. Paige, a pioneer in peace studies and the founder of the series of conferences in which we were participating, brought us together. Both of us take this opportunity to express our profound gratitude to him for having done so.

Since our initial encounter, we have met for dialogues on several occasions. We have discussed peace, our obvious common concern. In addition, our talks have taken the form of a dialogue on Buddhism, between a leader of a major Buddhist organization and a neophyte feeling his way into one of the richest, most life-enhancing bodies of thought in the world.

In the dialogue as it appears in this book, we search for ways of interfacing Buddhism and peace. To some of our readers, this attempt may seem abstract. Such, however, is not the case. Our search inspires very concrete, this-world proposals that are valid today, that will be useful in connection with the political agenda of tomorrow and that, had they been advanced, might have been useful yesterday or the day before.

We share a common basis. In Ikeda's case, this is deeply rooted in the Mahayana Buddhism of Nichiren Daishonin. In the case of Galtung, it started with Gandhi and developed toward a more general Buddhist orientation. In both instances, the basis requires that we perform concrete work in the world and between and within ourselves. Unless such work is inspired by a general conviction, however, it can become piece work instead of peace work.

There are many roads to peace. And we by no means maintain that ours is the only approach. But we do insist on the attainment of peace through peaceful means, which we are deeply convinced can be found, given a little foresight. Since such is our attitude, the reader will find in this book no recommendations for the use of violence or military force. Our proposals are in the nonviolent spirit of Shakyamuni Buddha (Siddhartha Gautama) and Gandhi. We devote a great deal of attention to the United Nations, which we hope will promote peace through peaceful means.

Wherever we look in the world today, we find un-peace. Some sadly unrealistic people believed that the Cold War was the only source of direct violence in the world. They thought that, once it was over, direct violence and even history itself would be over, too. Such people failed to understand that direct violence has two mighty sources capable of unleashing the violence potential in the human – particularly the male human – being.

One of those sources is the *structural violence* of repression and exploitation. Over 500 years ago, Christopher Columbus traveled too far. In doing so he opened the way for the global spreading of structural violence, which, though silent and only unintentionally harmful, has created a legacy that the white Christian West will have to cope with for many years to come. As a consequence of structural violence, inequity in the world is increasing. People generally dislike being repressed or exploited. And when they find themselves in such situations, they rebel, sometimes violently.

Cultural violence, the second source, legitimizes direct and structural violence by convincing people that, in the name of God or of history, they are not only justified but also duty-bound to harm or even kill others. Some religions, political ideologies and nation-alisms are moderate and tolerant. Others, however, place so high a premium on the self and so thoroughly dehumanize the other that, in the eyes of their adherents, massacre of the other seems an acceptable option.

During the Cold War, the East employed repression to counter exploitation and, in its very center, the Soviet Union, ended up deeply embedded in both. The West, on the other hand, used exploita-tion to overcome repression. It too ended up with both but cleverly burdened the periphery of its construction with all the costs. East and West were so thoroughly inspired by their ideologies – blueprints for Utopia – that both were willing to sacrifice a major part of humanity in a nuclear war directed against each other.

In the end, the East, which had suffered the costs of its own missionary zeal in its very center, imploded. The population rebelled, but did so nonviolently. The numerous rebellions that occurred, and still persist, on the periphery of the West are easily contained because they are distant from the center.

Distorted perceptions of reality are both causes and conse-quences of massive structural and cultural violence. No one is served by a vision so removed from reality that it becomes impossibly unreal or surrealist. Both utopian classless societies and free-market societies can cause the deaths of millions because they are too insuf-ficiently complex to accommodate the contradictions of human and social reality.

Buddhism seeks to combine a realistic insight into the contra-dictions of human life with an approach that has stood the test of time: meditation and dialogue for the sake of mutual improvement. These two processes may be referred to as the *inner* and the *outer* dialogue. The outer dialogue may take the form of a joint search, conducted around a conference table, for a way out of a given impasse. In such instances, two or more spirits help each other improve their joint karma, thus transcending any idea of predetermination.

Because it entails scrutinizing assumptions, laying them bare for others to see, the inner dialogue is equally important. Ideally, inner and outer dialogues should inspire each other. Rushing to have a conference before one's own assumptions about an issue have been examined can aggravate the situation. The inner dialogue that remains totally internal without being used in the quest for unity and peace is tainted with egocentrism. Taken together, however, the inner and outer dialogues are urgently needed tools of transcendence. When this happens, Buddhism and peace become two sides of the same coin and are accessible to all. We hope that our book will make a contribution in that direction.

Johan Galtung
Daisaku Ikeda

CHAPTER 1

Learning and Doing

Norway

IKEDA: Norway, your homeland, has a tradition of laudable humanistic achievements.

Highly symbolic of Norwegian humanism in diplomacy were the secret conferences that took place in your country between representatives of the government of Israel and the Palestine Liberation Organization (PLO) not long ago and that led to the signing of a tentative agreement on Palestinian autonomy. The venues of the meetings – in Foreign Minister Johan Holst's home and in a farmhouse – impressed me as especially warmly humane.

But humanism has long been a characteristic of the Norwegian people. For example, the Norwegian Arctic explorer Fridjof Nansen (1861–1930), who became the first high commissioner for refugees of the League of Nations, exerted himself valiantly on behalf of refugees the world over. In the chaotic period following World War I, he arranged for the repatriation of over half a million German and Austrian prisoners of war and of other refugees who had been forced to flee from their homelands. These efforts won him high praise and a Nobel peace prize. Norway did much to relieve the starvation and destitution that wracked Soviet Armenia after World War I. It seems significant that the Swedish philanthropist Alfred Nobel (1833–96) chose to have his prize for peace administered not in Sweden, but in Norway.

Is there anything particular in the Norwegian social or physical environment that stimulates humanistic concerns? Have you felt any influence of this kind on your own life?

GALTUNG: This is a difficult question for a Norwegian to answer. Peace must affect the whole globe, and Norway is only a small country, a remote province of the world. But it participates actively in all kinds of international organizations. Even our Viking ancestors – who became merchant mariners, later settling down but to some extent remaining imperialists – were in a sense world citizens.

Personally, I consider myself a citizen of the world, part of an all-embracing life that transcends humanity and includes past and

1

future. On my list of priorities, I put my Norwegian-ness below my
roles as peace activist and peace researcher.

Certainly Fridjof Nansen did the things you mention – and
more. But, like practically everyone else, he was ambiguous, as he
was also a Norwegian nationalist, sometimes dangerously close to
the kind of movement associated with another Norwegian, the
Nazi sympathizer and wartime puppet prime minister, Vidkun
Quisling (1887–1945).

I am not certain that instituting the Nobel peace prize in Norway
instead of in Sweden was complimentary to Norway. At the time,
the two countries were still unified under the same king. Whereas
Sweden was considered the mature, cosmopolitan, developed
region, Norway remained in a kind of early puberty, in a straitjacket
of national romanticism. Some people have interpreted Nobel's
decision as giving the soft prize to moralist Norway and retaining
the serious ones in scientific, modern Sweden.

Having said these things, however, I must admit that my homeland
has had a profound impact on me – an impact that others may detect
better than I can myself. For one thing, my inherited Norwegian
love of nature makes environmentalism come easy. We Norwegians
are – or once were – little impressed by the glitter of the world.
Norwegians have a sense of genuine equality and insist that respect
be conferred only on the deserving and not be associated with
position only. For instance, if someone – say the prime minister –
enters a room, we Norwegians do not bow subserviently. A prime
minister must demonstrate that he or she merits respect by doing
a good job. The position alone is only an empty shell.

Our pacifist views have been shaped by our largely egalitarian
inclinations and – just as important – by our having succeeded in
creating a confederation – a community of peaceful, egalitarian
Nordic countries – after centuries of the domination of small
nations like Iceland, Norway and Finland by powerful states such
as Denmark and Sweden. No doubt the relative lack of structural
and direct violence within and among those countries has inspired
a thesis to the effect that 'less structural violence will generally mean
less direct violence'.

I share neither the relative reticence and shyness nor the modesty
– genuine or false – of many Norwegians. Norway tends to chop
off the heads of those who stick out their necks to proclaim their
own knowledge; this is the flip-side of Norwegian equality. My own
fair, no doubt well-deserved, share of such treatment is one reason
why I often prefer to live outside my country of origin.

But my major reason for living outside Norway is the universal
scope of peace itself. Having been born in a community of about
4 million people, inhabiting one of the most beautiful lands on Earth,
does not limit the scope of my call of duty to my homeland.

Permit me at this point to express my gratitude to the Rinde family – remarkable business people – who exemplify Norwegian humanistic concern. In the 1950s they provided the funding necessary to found Norwegian social sciences in general and peace research in particular. Work in both fields has proved itself valuable enough to make funding available even for new and risky projects. Though peace research has had little or no impact on Norwegian foreign policy, the rich, fruitful, social-science milieu created in and around the Rinde-financed Institute for Social Research and its offshoot, the International Peace Research Institute in Oslo, has had an impact in other interesting ways, which I shall discuss later.

IKEDA: As you say, Norwegians are unimpressed by the glitter of the world, love nature and peace and seek nobility in human nature. No doubt these traits have been influenced by their environment. I cannot help thinking that the natural setting played a vital role in the actions of the Vikings and of great twentieth-century Norwegian explorers like Fridjof Nansen, Roald Amundsen and Thor Heyerdahl and in humane Norwegian policies toward refugees, immigrants and social issues. No doubt, too, harsh winters have encouraged the Norwegians to live in a practical, planned way. And this in turn has given birth to a social security system that is reputedly the best in the world.

Accepting Challenges

IKEDA: I have heard that seeing your beloved father, Dr August Galtung, a former deputy mayor of Oslo and a physician, taken away to a concentration camp by the Nazis when you were only 13 years old motivated you to devote yourself to humanitarianism and peace.

GALTUNG: My motivations were twofold. On the private level, I was influenced by the violent madness that afflicted Norway in general and our own small family in particular during World War II. I wanted to find out how all that horror might have been avoided; how the karma of all Europe might have been improved; and, in honest, personal terms, how we could have kept father at home with us.

Was the answer armed resistance or nonviolent self-protection? The answer certainly was not accepting violent occupation by the Nazis. The Norwegian people agonized over the choice at the time and, to a great extent, still do. We are said to be afflicted with what is called the April-the-ninth complex, named for the date of the German invasion of Norway: 9 April 1940.

My second motivation was quite different. Like most teenagers in modern societies, I was in search of a meaningful life-occupation, even some kind of mission. My search for a career lead me to consider being a physician, a chemist, a physicist, a sociologist and finally a peace researcher. The only problem was that the last profession did not exist at the time; it was a new area of study waiting to be created. This agonizing sequence involved parallel studies in two faculties: natural science and social science. The work was strenuous, but I regret none of it because it opened my mind to many per-spectives on science and the human condition.

Throughout my life, I have tried to adopt the policy of accepting, instead of passing up, challenges. My underlying assumption is the simple belief that we grow through challenges, that one challenge prepares us for the next. Certainly I have found – and still find – work in the name of peace more than sufficiently challenging. Response to this challenge has led me to set as one of my goals the development of practicable theories of peace and conflict.

My motivations, then, were of both the head and the heart. Refusing to regard them as mutually exclusive, I interpret them as existing in a yin–yang relationship; that is, there is a brain function within the heart and a heart function within the brain. Full attention must be paid to both at all levels. For this, much inner dialogue is needed.

My heart yearned for peace, which my head did not know how to achieve. And my head went astray because it was insufficiently guided by my heart. After years of agony, preparation and waiting, during the 1950s I embarked on the first, modest projects. The ultimate answer to my quest for a mission came in the form of peace research, a field of endeavor that I had the honor of helping to bring into being as a university discipline. It is now gaining increasing respect.

IKEDA: I am in full agreement with accepting challenges, which do indeed enable us to grow and prepare for still further challenges. In *Faust*, which I have loved since my youth, the poet Goethe (1749–1832) says that, as long as they go on striving, human beings will go astray. Effort expended in overcoming challenges, however, stimulates reform by subjecting us to a tempering process of trial-and-error struggles with reality. My own awareness of the stimulation and growth resulting from accepting challenges deepened when, at the age of 19, I came into contact with Buddhism and began my own struggle in the name of peace.

It saddens me to see that many young people today lack the courage to accept challenges. Adopting know-it-all attitudes, they remain apparently content with their circumstances. But this approach brings no true contentment. The imperishable treasures of experience and true satisfaction are obtained only by people who set goals for themselves and challenge all obstacles in the way of their attainment.

The impact of the personality of my mentor, Josei Toda (1900–58), played a vital role in inspiring me to accept Buddhism and face the challenge of taking Buddhist teachings of peace to the whole world. But there were other contributory factors as well. One was my own personal hatred of war, developed as a consequence of our family's suffering during World War II and of my mother's grief at my older brother's death in battle in Burma. Another was my search for a belief that would serve the need of humanity and peace, especially at a time when Japanese youth was experiencing the spiritual vacuum caused by the collapse of traditional values. Just as I was making this search, I encountered Buddhism, a religion that truly strives for peace and the good of humanity.

Carrying out my religious task has taught me a great deal about human strength and weakness, nobility and pettiness, wisdom and folly. All my experiences in this field have tempered me and deepened my certainty in the value of Buddhism.

Today, Soka Gakkai International is poised to soar aloft in the noble effort to make Buddhism the religion of peace for all peoples. I am resolved to devote the rest of my life to facing all challenges related to this endeavor.

Philosophers from the Masses

IKEDA: You have met and known leading world figures in many nations. Your contacts and interactions with peoples in all walks of life must have suggested numerous ideas for solving the problems facing humankind today and for achieving lasting global peace.

GALTUNG: Like everyone who is deeply involved in the affairs of nations, I have met my share of presidents, vice-presidents, prime ministers and foreign ministers. They are, by and large, just like everybody else. Of course, because they must be attractive enough to get their way without resorting to excessive violence, they are often long on charm, radiance and rhetorical ability. The ruthless dictator needs less of these persuasive qualities than an elected leader. We must be careful to note, however, that dictators may be more honest, since they have no need to conceal their ruthlessness.

Some of the high-placed people I have met are knowledgeable, imaginative, compassionate; many are not. It is commonly held that such people have one thing in common: they are greedy for power and lack substance and legitimacy. I am not sure that political leaders have a monopoly on these traits, which I have found among all kinds of people, from professors to plumbers. Many politicians take power for granted, as if they had been born to it; others struggle hard to attain it. The more they struggle, the less real power they seem to obtain. Often all they have are the symbols of power.

Postwar Third World leaders such as Kwame Nkrumah, Fidel Castro, Julius Nyerere and the Dalai Lama impressed me enormously. Eager as they are to maintain their global grip, leaders of the First World, no matter what their generation, tend to repress and exploit rather than liberate and develop and so impress me less.

Perhaps my background in life and training as a sociologist have given me a greater sensitivity to the common people than political or philosophical inclination alone could have inspired. In my day, Norway demanded that conscientious objectors, of which I was one, fulfill an extra six months of civic service. I refused, unless that service was meaningful in some way for peace. As a result of my refusal, the Norwegian courts imprisoned me for six months. This experience brought me into contact with heroes in the struggle for day-to-day survival. I have had similar experiences all over the Third World, especially among women and in Latin America and South Asia, the two Third World regions I know best. These people all impressed me deeply. Others I might mention are people who take powerful, nonviolent action, like pacifist women in East and West Europe who were very instrumental in bringing an end to the Cold War.

IKEDA: I share your sense of identification with the common people. Once during an informal talk with some business people, a member of the group commented on the extent to which I travel – much more extensively, he said, than he and his colleagues – and asked what attitude I adopt when meeting someone new.

I unhesitatingly replied that people are as different as they are numerous. Some are high placed, like heads of state; some are immensely erudite; and some are enormously rich. But, like everyone else, the high-placed, learned and wealthy are inevitably subject to the Buddhist Four Sufferings: birth, aging, illness and death. No one can avoid them. Because in this sense we are all equal, I attempt to disregard exteriors and approach all people as fundamentally equal.

The truly great members of the masses of humanity are the people who labor not in the spotlight, but behind the scenes. I am most comfortable and can work most untiringly in the company of philosophers from the masses.

I treasure many profound, unostentatious comments that I have heard from such people. Nor am I alone in this. The famous American philosopher and psychologist William James (1842–1910) said that the most impressive words of philosophy he ever heard came from the mouth of an uneducated repairman doing work at his house: 'When you come right down to it, the differences separating people are very small but very important.'

Learning from Giants

IKEDA: Among the people whose works you have studied or among the human beings you have known personally, whom do you consider to have been most influential on your thought?

GALTUNG: As a young student, I was very much attracted to the humanism – and faith in humanity – of the Dutch-Jewish philosopher Baruch Spinoza (1632–77). His thought bridges the moral and the cognitive. For instance, he says that lack of understanding produces evil whereas understanding brings good. My own faith in peace research may derive from the idea that, in addition to other ways, there is a cognitive, intellectual road to peace. Because it is helpful to know what actions will help us find that way, presenting the maximum number of nonviolent alternatives to conflict is a major task of peace research. We must always be constructive and always propose as many alternatives as possible, because one day the ideas of a better world we plant in the hearts and minds of the people with whom we come into contact will become reality.

Obviously I regard Mohandas Gandhi (1869–1948) as a great influence – a giant for all times. Two of the most impressive aspects of his personality were optimism and imagination. Preaching the axioms of nonviolence is easy; believing in nonviolence strongly enough to devise practicable ways to make it work and then making it work are much more difficult.

Equally impressive in Gandhi was his Asian – in his case, Hindu-Buddhist – way of avoiding the false dichotomies that enslave many Western intellectuals and politicians. As an example, I might mention just one of those dichotomies: that between leftism and rightism.

Whereas people of the rightist persuasion consider it essential to oppose direct violence by building barriers in the form of hierarchies, deterrence, police and military laws, those of leftist views insist it is necessary to overthrow such structural violence by permitting the minimum – or maximum – of direct violence involved in revolution. Gandhi was against both direct and structural violence and fought for their reduction through his splendid doctrines of *satyagraha* (the force born of truth) and *sarvodaya* (the uplifting of all). In other words, he avoided both the leftist and the rightist pitfalls by fighting the structural violence of colonialism, caste and racism nonviolently.

I am forever grateful to my philosophy teacher at the University of Oslo, Professor Arne Naess, for introducing me simultaneously to Spinoza and Gandhi. (I was 22 and Professor Naess 41 at the time.) Professor Naess was and remains a world-famous specialist in both. It is always best to learn from giants. A small Buddhist treatise bearing the stamp of the Lord Buddha is more inspiring than everything printed in the social science journals. Of course, I do not mean that the two kinds of writing are mutually exclusive.

Another person whose work as a social scientist I found deeply influential was Pitirim Sorokin (1889–1968), a Russian/Komi sociologist who left Russia after the revolution to live and teach in the United States. No matter how many times I read it, his *Social and Cultural Dynamics* always has something new to offer. Too great for his contemporaries, this genius will probably not be fully appreciated until the next century. He possessed a tremendous capacity for synthesizing vast regions of knowledge and for discovering rhythms in the histories of civilizations by holding these syntheses up to time. From the days of his political activities with Alexander Kerensky (1881–1970; leader of the provisional government after the March Revolution of 1917) in Petrograd until his life at Harvard, Sorokin was a true child of Western civilization, to which, however, he held up a warning mirror.

No doubt I owe much of my passion for macro-history and analysis of civilizations to Sorokin. When I had the honor of meeting him, late in his life, lack of due recognition had marked and marred him too much. The West did not welcome his warnings, especially as, in the depths of the depressed 1930s, he foresaw major catastrophes and the absurd extremes toward which the materialist – or 'sensate', as he called it – culture was headed.

IKEDA: The most deeply influential person in my life was Josei Toda, my mentor and the second president of Soka Gakkai. When I first met him, he was 47 and I was 19. The occasion was a lecture on 'The Philosophy of Life', held at the home of a friend from primary-school days.

The assembly room was packed with poorly dressed but wonderfully animated middle-aged men, housewives and young people. In the midst of them, a man with a prominent forehead and thick glasses was talking in a carefree manner. It was Mr Toda.

While discussing Buddhism, he avoided a preaching tone and conventional philosophical language. By means of familiar examples, he perceptively talked about daily life and contemporary politics. Though brusque, his manner of speaking radiated indescribable warmth.

At the end of the lecture, my friend introduced me to Mr Toda, who smiled most sociably as he spoke to me. I immediately confronted him with all my doubts about the best way to live, the nature of true patriotism, the merits and demerits of the Japanese emperor system, the quintessence of Buddhism and so on. His lucid replies went directly to the heart of matters without affectation or meandering. The truths I had been seeking emerged immediately and in vibrant forms. I was at once deeply moved and satisfied by what I heard. This encounter with the rare personality of Josei Toda caused my life to shift into gear in a big way.

Later I went to work for the publishing house Mr Toda ran. A stubborn economic recession then plaguing Japan spelled serious trouble for his business too. Salaries were in arrears; employees quit, one after the other. But I was resigned to stay by his side to the last.

At about this time, I was obliged to give up my studies in order to help both in rebuilding Mr Toda's businesses and in restructuring Soka Gakkai, which had suffered greatly during World War II. In order that my education should not be neglected, Mr Toda offered to teach me himself.

For a number of years, at his house or early in the morning at the office, he tutored me in an astonishing array of subjects, including law, politics, economics, astronomy, classical Chinese, Buddhism and modern philosophy. Sometimes, worn out from negotiating with creditors, I would oversleep and dash into the office late. He was always there, waiting for me.

As you say, it is good to learn from giants. For me and many others, Josei Toda was a giant. His own conduct provided the model for a kind of training for which I would then have gladly risked my life. I still feel the same way. Throughout my work for Buddhist-inspired world peace and along all the uncharted paths I have followed, Josei Toda has never left my thoughts for a moment.

I was deeply impressed by what you said about Pitirim Sorokin and the way his book *Social and Cultural Dynamics* preserves its appeal for you. As a young man, I tended to devote myself to the philosophy of one great book at a time. At one period, that work was the *Essais* of Michel de Montaigne (1533–92). In Japan, after World War II, we young people frantically sought new beliefs to replace failed older ones. A few of us book-lovers formed a small reading group to help us in our search. Although of course many books had been destroyed in the war, we assembled whatever we could find and spent hours reading and talking. We discussed Montaigne's thoughts on fate endlessly. The idea that happiness or unhappiness is determined not by fate but by what we ourselves, using willpower and determination, do with the raw materials of life was a source of intense inspiration.

Opening the Door

IKEDA: As a prodigious and widely quoted author yourself, I suspect you are an avid reader as well.

GALTUNG: I might cite the work of two authors. First is the Norwegian Nini Roll Anker (1873–1942). Obviously reading her book *Kvinnen og den svarte fuglen* (The Woman and the Black Bird) is not essential to the development of a pacifist or a conscientious objector, but it helps. Her broad theme is the insanity of World War I. The victims she describes are not the dead but the almost mortally wounded who, denied the blessed escape of death, survived as what we today refer to as human vegetables. Ignorant, unimaginative and totally compassionless so-called statesmen sent these soon-to-be victims into battle to kill or be killed. The author's more particular theme is a woman's struggle to recall her own wounded son to life and her awakening to political consciousness.

The other author is Henrik Ibsen (1828–1906). Of course, I draw on my own culture for inspiration and sustenance and cannot imagine what being Norwegian would be like without Ibsen – no doubt Norway's greatest gift to the world.

In *En folkefiende* (An Enemy of the People), a doctor named Stockmann has the courage to stand up not only against the government – as we all occasionally must in a democracy – but also against a solid majority of the citizenry. He calls their bluff and condemns their ignorance and greed. Ibsen was actually writing about the environmental crisis that came a century after his time and that has become one of the major problems of our own time. He could easily have written about the other problems: misery and war, social disintegration and alienation.

Like my beloved father – who taught me the triangle diagnosis–prognosis–therapy when I was still a child – Stockmann in *En folkefiende* is a doctor confronting people who, far from being submissive, sick patients, are unamenable to all his advice. Even when I was only 14 or 15, Dr Stockmann impressed me greatly, as did two other of Ibsen's great characters: Peer Gynt, who constantly fools himself, and Brand, who demands much too much of other people. Among Norwegians, as among all other peoples, there are many representatives of both types. I can trace something of all three of these men in myself – Stockmann and Peer Gynt and Brand, too.

IKEDA: Ibsen is a towering figure in Western literature as well as a spiritual treasure and monument for the people of Norway. He is widely known and read in the East too. The eminent Japanese poet and novelist Toson Shimazaki (1872–1943) wrote an evaluation of

Ibsen as a person. Members of the reading group I mentioned earlier used to read Ibsen, particularly *Et dukkehjem* (A Doll's House).

In connection with my own deep conviction of the importance of the 'human revolution', I feel strong sympathy with something Ibsen wrote in one of his letters:

> We have been living on crumbs dropped from the revolution-ary table of the preceding century. They have been chewed far too long. Thought requires new nourishment and stimulus. *Liberté, Egalité et Fraternité* no longer mean what they meant in the age of the guillotine.
>
> Bullheaded politicians make no effort to understand this. That is why I hate them. All they want is a political revolution, a particular revolution superficial in all things. Such a revolution is absurd. The important thing is renovation of the human spirit.

In spite of their emphasis on renovation of the human spirit and the need to provide the age with new nourishment and stimulus, Ibsen's plays did not initially find a ready market. Businessmen opposed their publication. The satirical magazine he edited was forced to close. His theatrical innovations were frustrated. And for a long time he met with little but misfortune.

Even after they had attained recognition, his plays were practi-cally always greeted with as much adverse as favorable comment. Instead of being discouraged, however, Ibsen used criticism as inspi-ration for new ideas and plays that served to refute his critics' complaints. His stylistic versatility is so great that no two of his 25 plays employ the same techniques.

In *An Enemy of the People*, Dr Stockmann attempts to halt pollution of a hot-springs town and is removed from his position by townspeople who refuse to understand his intentions (these people are spiritually as polluted as the hot springs). But in the final scene, Stockmann says to his family, 'I've made a great discovery. The strongest thing in the world is a man who stands alone.' I cannot help thinking that Stockmann's final lines represent Ibsen's own call for a spiritual renovation of the masses.

In my own novel, *The Human Revolution*, I depict the postwar life of my mentor Josei Toda and show how, after leaving prison, where he had been unjustly confined for his religious work, he struggled alone for reconstruction in the ruins of his homeland. The German poet Schiller (1759–1805) said that true heroism requires one to be strong, even though standing alone. Stockmann and Josei Toda were true heroes in Schiller's sense.

GALTUNG: Do you believe that literature and art have the power to bind human beings together and to strengthen the Buddha nature within us?

IKEDA: Art binds the minds of people together and is a fundamental force opening up brilliant prospects for the future of humanity. In 'Poetry – A Prospect for Humanity', a paper I submitted to the tenth World Poets' Conference, held in 1988, I said that poetry is the spiritual bond between human beings, society and the universe. And in a speech entitled 'Art and Spirituality in the East and West', which I delivered before the Institut de France in 1989, I spoke of the bonding power of art.

All phenomena are constantly mutating in keeping with strict laws. Sometimes fusing, sometimes dispersing, they generate both consonances and dissonances. Their resonances and reverberations evolve the great drama of life. Art and literature have the power to reflect that drama in all its sweep and brilliance. Among humanity's noblest fields of endeavor, they open the door to the limitless happiness, compassion and wisdom with which universal life is replete and bring us closer to the power of creativity.

Contact with superior art makes us feel one with all humanity, the world of nature and the universe. Works of art are expressions of the individuals and peoples of the times in which they are created. They are hymns of the soul and fruits of the actions of people who have been inspired by contacts with the universal life. Coming into contact with great literature, paintings or music evokes profound emotions – feelings of fulfillment and joy at knowing our lives to be stimulated and expanded by the exquisite rhythms of the universal life.

Because he knew this, Josei Toda urged us to read and familiarize ourselves with the works of the great artists. He was always interested in our progress in these fields and, until shortly before he died, often questioned me about my reading.

Sharing with others contact with the rhythms of the universal life through appreciation of great works of art generates spiritual solidarity that can be expanded to link all peoples everywhere. Experiencing art helps us rediscover our true humanity and return to that elemental life where we are all on a footing of equality, where no barriers exist. In a very real sense, art and literature are tools for peace because the knowledge and experience gained from appreciating and sharing them cultivate nonviolence, compassion, trust, solidarity, beauty and breadth of mind, and intensified awareness of the natures and needs of all humanity.

Ways of Learning

IKEDA: As the founder of Soka University, I consider education one of the most important aspects of our preparations for the future. Indicative of your own devotion to education is your program entitled 'Peace Studies around the World', in connection with which you brought 35 students to Japan in the spring of 1990. Obviously you have a firm grasp on the most salient aspects of educating the young.

GALTUNG: Education should be primarily self-education. Second in importance to self-education is co-education, in the sense of communal exchanges of views and experiences among friends and colleagues who are on the same level of development – extended self-education, so to speak, or a colloquium involving mutual tutoring. Important, but not decisive, is other-education; that is the teacher–pupil, professor–student, *sensei–seito* relation. I ascribe to this third category no more than perhaps 10 per cent of the total. But those 10 per cent are important.

The English word 'educate' derives from Latin *educare*, which contains the root *dux*, or leader, which in turn occurs in Mussolini's title *il Duce*, the Italian counterpart of the German *der Führer*. To educate is thought by some to consist of leading children, even against their will, into adulthood. In accordance with this interpretation, teachers see themselves striving to evoke certain effects in students. Though this process is widely applied and to an extent indispensable, I remain skeptical about it. The educator seeks to be the cause of effects produced in others. This in my view is too asymmetrical a relationship; it involves too much power and almost constitutes violence.

In school and at university, I listened to teachers, more or less attentively, and then started forming my own questions independently. Next I searched exploringly, sometimes alone and sometimes in endless discussions with other students, for answers to my questions. Every day for four or five years, a very good friend and I discussed the topics uppermost in our minds for a couple of hours on our way home from school. The same kind of talks occupied much of my time at university. I still continue this practice and will never give it up.

All three kinds of education are limitless. In later age, however, the range of discussion partners may narrow, unless the individual sees in every other person – as I try to do – a potential for mutual enrichment. The danger always exists of ending up with only professors in one's own field as dialogue partners.

Pedagogy – the word contains the root *ped*, derived from Greek *pais*, or child – entails the teacher–student relationship. The teacher brings students either to a high or a low temperature of enthusiasm. I disapprove of the usual university practice – undeniably convenient from the administrators' viewpoint – of holding lectures for a given course at a fixed hour on isolated days of the week. By the time the teacher works his or her students up to a point of interest or enthusiasm, class is over. Work on the topic will not be resumed for, at best, two more days and perhaps not until the following week. Usually, by the end of the class hour, students have already shifted their attention to the next course. For students and teachers alike, exclusive devotion to one topic for at least a week is a much better system because it makes possible the kind of immersion students experience in modern intensive language courses. Surely no one would countenance doing away with such language courses on the basis of no more than administrative convenience. The same should be true of intensive teaching in other fields as well.

Only when class activities inspire high pedagogical temperatures does inspiration grow intense enough for students to take off on their own and initiate courses of self-education or co-education to supplement teacher–student pedagogy. I have tried to create conditions of this kind under various circumstances, especially during my period as director-general of the Inter-university Center in Dubrovnik, Croatia. One-day seminars can be useful too. The important point is to combine exposure, communication, dialogue and concentration as intensively as possible. (This topic will be explored in more detail in a forthcoming book, *Education for Peace and Development*.)

'Peace Studies around the World', which you kindly mention, was an extreme example of implementing the kind of learning circumstances I advocate. In this program, 35 students from ten countries lived together for eight months, sharing everything, including the services of 288 excellent lecturers in the 20 nations we visited. We stayed longer in some countries than in others; for instance, we were a full month each in China, Japan and Hawaii. Though a tremendous experience, the program required maturity and was therefore too demanding for some of the students. Furthermore, it was necessary for the requisite maturity to have been developed beforehand, because the program was too intense to allow it to evolve only during the course. The emotional temperature generated by the teaching was very high, and some students got burned.

All these reflections on other- , self- and co-education as an eternal dialectic are subsumed in the importance of experiencing the world. In the classroom, it is possible to sense immediately which students have opened themselves to reality. Travel is not indispensable to this openness, though it helps, especially travel as experienced by young people today: hiking, working their way around, camping, making expeditions, taking summer courses and staying with families in other countries. Mere tourism from point A to point B and back is insufficient. In fact, it is deficient, often creating a distorted view instead of uplifting and enriching the mind.

The inner dialogue – or meditation – is also a highly self-educating process that may take many forms. A person may meditate seated in front of a wall in a Buddha position. But it is equally possible to meditate while walking, bicycling, or traveling by land or sea. The changing sea-, land- and city-scapes that appear, alter and vanish from consciousness as one travels by train or ship inspire and supply metaphors for thoughts and ideas. I do not find travel by airplane equally inspiring.

To sum up, *meditation* and inner dialogue should play a bigger role in education than *mediation* on the part of teachers and instructors. The difference in the spelling of the two words is slight, but the difference between their meanings is enormous.

IKEDA: Your attitude toward the role of the instructor reminds me of a comment in the writings of Nichiren Daishonin (1222–82), founder of Nichiren Buddhism: 'To teach another something is like oiling the wheels of a heavy cart so that they will turn, or like floating a boat upon the water so that it may move ahead without difficulty' (*The Major Writings of Nichiren Daishonin*, vol. 5, p. 307). Fundamentally, education must be the process of evoking latent potentials and must always respect the child's individual personality and limitless potentialities. The French historian Philippe Ariès (1914–84) speaks of what he calls the 'discovery of the child', by which he means the realization that children are more than miniature adults and require special treatment geared to their abilities and needs.

Too often, in all parts of the world, children have been treated like miniature adults. In medieval Europe, after infancy, children were expected to play adultlike roles in many different fields of endeavor. Special terminology to describe children did not emerge in Europe before the fourteenth century; and it was not until the sixteenth century that clothing, toys and books specifically designed for children began to make an appearance. The idea of an age of childhood did not evolve in France and the rest of Europe until after the seventeenth century.

Before the second half of the nineteenth century and the evolution of a modern Japanese state, Japanese education consisted of what was called *koyarai*, or pushing children into society from behind. This is the very opposite of the modern educational idea of recognizing children as immature and trying to coax them forward from a leadership position.

The recurrence in East and West of similar educational ideas suggests that both occidental and oriental approaches regarded children as incomplete or semi-human beings. The tendency to overemphasize the acquisition of knowledge at the expense of understanding seems to be rooted in this attitude.

Because relations between children and adults and between children and the family change very slowly, improvements in educational methods and systems must be long-term and sound. All attempts at cheap tricks or mere bright ideas that ignore children's peculiar needs are doomed to fail. This is why I feel that your emphasis on high interest-temperatures and experience is most meaningful. I see similarities between it and the ideas of Tsunesaburo Makiguchi (1871–1944), a brilliant Japanese educator and the first president of Soka Gakkai, who advocated a half-day school system. He believed that students should spend half the day in class and devote the remainder to productive work or specialized learning consonant with their individual abilities and interests. In his view, instead of being a preparation for life, learning should take place simultaneously with real-life working situations. Moreover, he believed this course should be pursued throughout life.

He proposed using schools and faculty labor forces on a two- or three-shift basis in order to accommodate more students, reduce costs and improve efficiency. His system would have the additional advantage of ameliorating the Japanese system of examinations, universally condemned as the 'examination hell'. It would dramatically reduce the amount of factual information to be memorized for examinations and then forgotten forever.

Certainly I agree wholeheartedly with your estimation of the value to education of internal dialogue and actual experience. Nonetheless, traditional institutes of education too have important roles to play. For one thing, today, as practical steps toward building an enduring peace become more vital than ever before, we must train specialists to advise us about what to do, how and when to do it, and how to make our measures as effective as possible. Much of this training must be done in conventional institutions of higher learning.

GALTUNG: Specialists must have high ideals, respect life and believe firmly in the possibilities inherent in humanity. Buddhism and the soft, nonviolent power aspects of Gandhi-ism provide significant sources of the abilities and attitudes we need. I should like to know what Soka University can do to accelerate the cultivation of such specialists.

IKEDA: I identify two major aspects of peace-creating: the ethical and the rational, policy-determining aspects. Specialist wisdom is especially vital to the latter. We must train people who share the pacifist philosophy with the general population and who provide information essential to policy decisions. As its founder, I recognize and wish to support Soka University's many possibilities in this connection. When the institution was founded, I suggested as one element of its spiritual basis the will to act as a fortress guarding peace for all humanity and urged the adoption of humanity-oriented education, culture and peace as the three pillars of its philosophy. I earnestly hope that the university will direct its essential educational activities toward the cultivation of peace specialists.

GALTUNG: I share that hope. Today peace studies are evolving from a focus on building knowledge (peace research), to an emphasis on skills (peace training). Soka University could play a leading role in this connection.

Realists of the Head; Idealists of the Heart

IKEDA: The Japanese tend to regard the Vikings as pirates and marauders and often overlook the important role they played in trade throughout the Western world. Proverbial Viking courage could only have evolved in harsh conditions; as the Scandinavian saying has it, 'The Vikings were born of the north wind.' Perhaps parents and educators should strive harder to cultivate an undaunted spirit in the younger generations of today in order to help them confront life's north winds as courageously as the Vikings did.

GALTUNG: As with so much in this world, there were two sides to the Vikings. After all, they were the authors of the wonderful, melancholy, darkly fatalistic Icelandic sagas, written in powerful Old Norse, the common ancestor language of northern Europe. But marauders contemptuous of vulnerable land-based people and their culture they certainly were too. In their early period, quick and agile, they believed in the philosophy of hit-and-run. Later, however, when they began living on taxes exacted from their victims, they grew flabby and lazy. Decline and fall were in the offing.

The imperialists of their day, the Vikings subjected other peoples to their will, for instance in Russia, where the very word *rus* is of Norse origin. As has been described by a horrified Arab historian named Ibn Fadlan, they were uncivilized, brutish, greedy and exploitative. At the same time, they were undeniably courageous and possessed of an undaunted spirit.

As you suggest, developing such traits in young people is important. But from my viewpoint, intense curiosity and compassion are more important still. It always has been, is and always will be better to search for positive, constructive and communal elements than to dwell only on the negative, bellicose and destructive. Of course, we must not ignore the negative and disharmonious. We must understand them completely, even to the painful point where we recognize that we ourselves are part not of the solutions, but of the problems. No one, of any age group, however, should confine awareness to negative elements. Instead we must all strive to transcend the negative in the quest for human unity and peace.

We must be realists in our brains while keeping the flame of idealism burning in our hearts. That is what peace research and peace-oriented action are about. Being blind to realities helps no one. By the same token, people who cannot develop a humane idealism transcending realism cannot contribute to the progress of humankind. People without this ability are preprogrammed – mainly by themselves – to repeat realistic rituals, prejudices and discrimination. Theirs is the profound pessimism of direct and structural violence. Their worst-case scenarios all too easily become self-fulfilling prophecies.

IKEDA: During his childhood, my friend and dialogue partner the author Chingiz Aitmatov, who was born in Kirgizia in the former Soviet Union, lost his father in the Stalinist purges. Thereafter his life was very cruel. But no matter how desperate his situation, he always clung hopefully to his ideals and never forgot the words of a village primary-school teacher who once admonished him to feel no shame over his father.

Aitmatov realizes the discrepancy between ideals and realities, but never permits it to make him either a desperate recluse or a visionary. He manages to keep a firm hold on both the realistic and the idealist reins by which he has guided his life. In 1991, in an interview for the *Frankfurter Allgemeine Zeitung*, he was asked to describe the greatest misfortune in life. Aitmatov refused, saying, 'I'm superstitious. If I answer this question, what I say may come true.' Of course, he was being humorous. But there is more to his refusal than mere humor. Behind a warm, friendly laugh, he was concealing all of his past bitter experiences, which no doubt in his mind's eye overlapped kaleidoscopically with his image of the future. This combination of warmth and composure are charac-teristic of Aitmatov, who contrasts sharply with the kind of person you describe as incapable of developing beyond realism. It takes a cool head and a warm heart to bring anything to maturity. As you say, 'We must be realists in our brains while keeping the flame of idealism burning in our hearts.'

Works Speak Louder than Words

IKEDA: As an activist peace scholar, instead of shutting yourself up in an ivory tower you visit trouble spots all over the world, trying to discover what can be done to rectify injustices. In an interview on Radio Moscow, I once said that action is much more important than mere conceptual talk about peace. My motto in this connection is: 'Don't just talk peace; work for it.'

GALTUNG: I have been greatly inspired by Gandhi's remark that 'There is no way to peace, peace is the way.' Under the influence of the same idea, some years ago when asked to summarize in four words the purpose of pacifist research, education and action, I came up with 'Peace by peaceful means.'

Gandhi's approach to ethical problems was empirical, even experimental. So was that of the famous scientist Albert Einstein (1879–1955). A moral injunction, such as the doctrine of non-violence, must be tested against empirical realities, which, in spite of our altering perceptions of them, do not themselves change. Gandhi's firm belief in nonviolence was born not only of high principles such as the Hindu-Buddhist unity of life, but also from the discovery that nonviolence works. Like the people who had experimented with democracy centuries, even millennia, before him, he experimented with nonviolence. Both Gandhi and Einstein were pragmatic, if not 100 per cent pragmatic.

For them, as for me, ethical norms cannot escape the test of reality. There is something almost Anglo-Saxon, Nordic and perhaps even Sino-Japanese in this truth. The world of the rational, whether it serves to anchor moral beliefs or general assumptions about reality, in no way excludes the sensually experienced empirical world, which, though necessary, is insufficient in itself. Gandhi bridged the gap between the two.

IKEDA: I am completely in accord with you when you speak of 'Peace through peaceful means'. Goethe said it is no good to keep our eyes only on goals in the distance. Each step along the way must be a goal in itself and have its own value. In your terms, this means that instead of aiming for peace as a faraway ideal, we must make each step we take in the direction of the goal represent peace.

It is a great absurdity of the human race to engage in war after war and to commit violence after violence in the noble name of peace. No matter what the goal, we must never resort to ethically unjustifiable means.

In this connection, I recall how Goethe declared that the havoc it wrought prevented him from sympathizing with the French Revolution, or indeed with any violent revolution. Without condemning revolution as such, he found intolerable the wanton destruction that inevitably accompanies whatever good violent revolutions accomplish. As Goethe pointed out, changes in the world of nature occur in their proper seasons. Roses bloom in June. Violent, extravagant change was as alien to his character as it is to nature itself.

With his customary perspicacity, Gandhi saw the violence inherent in revolution. During the so-called Red Thirties, when people disillusioned with the deepening injustices of unbridled capitalism were turning hopefully to socialism and the Soviet Union, the Mahatma put his finger on the Bolsheviks' great failing; that is, their condoning of violence. In a way, he prophesied the downfall of the Soviet Union.

In saying that ethical norms cannot escape the test of reality and that the rational in no way excludes the sensually experienced empirical world, you echo the sentiments of Goethe and Gandhi and indicate the need to look the truth of history in the face.

Optimists

IKEDA: You speak impressively of your mother's influence in cultivating in you the confirmed optimism to believe that any problem – including, in your case, the Nazi occupation, a father in a concentration camp and sisters gone abroad as refugees – can be overcome. When I was a child and our family business fell on hard times, my mother, too, remained courageously optimistic. She often said that if we were paupers, we were champion paupers. As I grow older, I realize more and more how greatly her indomitable cheerfulness and willpower inspired all of us.

The French philosopher Émile-August Chartier Alain (1868–1951) said that whereas pessimism arises from the disposition, optimism is born of the will. Confirmed optimists always believe in their own convictions and in tomorrow. Their optimism inspires and attracts others. It stimulates determination to overcome all obstacles on the path of ultimate victory.

GALTUNG: I consider pessimism to be a personal, self-indulgent luxury that none of us can afford. Certainly there are plenty of reasons inside and outside ourselves for pessimism. These reasons must not be rejected or overlooked and cannot be wished away. They must, however, be dealt with. The challenge must be accepted.

My own preferred formula for dealing with them is this: we must be pessimists with our brains and optimists with our hearts. Optimism and pessimism must constantly challenge each other in our daily, everlasting, internal dialogues. But if either is allowed to dominate completely, the process of challenge itself will fail.

A leader of a peace movement must radiate optimistic confidence in the existence of peaceful solutions to our dilemmas. But this confidence must be more than mere assurances, pledges and 'trust me' talk. It must be backed up with solid reasoning. True social reform leaders – like Danilo Dolci in the Sicily of the 1950s or Jayaprakash Narayan in the India of the 1960s – do more than merely walk with their followers, like a shepherd with a flock. Even in the most hopeless situations, they diagnose, they prognosticate, they devise therapies. Optimism as a general inclination is insufficient: optimism must be based on good reasons.

Two optimistic politicians whom I admire are Frederik W. de Klerk of South Africa, and Mikhail Sergeyevich Gorbachev. De Klerk's having managed to navigate a perilous minefield with minimum – at least so far – violence indicates true political greatness. To our immense good fortune, his life coincides with that of Nelson Mandela, himself a man of gigantic significance. We shall return later to Gorbachev, whom I also consider a gift to humanity.

The civil rights campaigner Martin Luther King, Jr. (1929–68) identified the source of optimism when he said, 'I have a dream.' The important thing is not the beauty of the vision but a firm conviction in the attainability of the vision, even from the present point in time and space and even when the outlook seems hopeless.

Whole peoples may be inspired by visions, as the native Hawaiians have been. A century has passed since, in 1893, a group of mostly American businessmen overthrew the Hawaiian monarchy, thus setting in motion the process that led to annexation by the US in 1898 and statehood in 1959. Since white people arrived on the islands, an original native population of 800,000 is said to have dwindled to about 8,000: genocide can be said to have taken place. Nonetheless, the Hawaiians preserve their vision of some day completely controlling parts of the islands. Growing numbers of native Hawaiians take pride in their indigenous tradition and compare themselves with the Native Americans on the mainland. Some of them want the islands to become an independent, multi-cultural nation, a home to all kinds of Hawaiians – Hawaiian Hawaiians, Japanese Hawaiians, American Hawaiians and so on.

Some day, the magnetic force of a well-evolved, well-dreamed, well-thought vision may help them attain that goal. But this will not come to pass merely because, as the saying goes, the right time has arrived. To speak of a vision whose time has come is nonsense. Time does not sneak up from behind us. We create subjective, organic time (*kairos*). Objective, physical time (*khronos*) is the affair of the stars and atomic clocks – so far, at least.

Humor is another source of optimism. Whereas tears, anxieties and fears may bring on apathy and despondency, smiles energize. But humor must be used with care. It is easy to neutralize issues by joking about them.

IKEDA: Your interesting comment about pessimists of the mind and optimists of the heart is in line with the ideas of the French philosopher Blaise Pascal (1623–62) on harmony between head and heart, the compatibility of enthusiasm and skepticism, and the geometric spirit and the delicate spirit.

You mention President de Klerk and Mikhail S. Gorbachev – a gift to humanity, in your words. To my good fortune, I have had the opportunity of meeting and sharing discussions with both.

During our meeting, in June 1992, President de Klerk and I spoke of the importance of dialogue. He considers dialogue of the very first importance and emphasizes interpersonal relations. One of his mottoes in fact is: 'I want to be your friend.' When in Israel he said that, in dealing with people from other countries, no matter who they are, he insists that initiating dialogue is the only way to establish peaceful ties. During our meeting, he reiterated this belief. Realizing that deep-rooted mistrust is one of South Africa's greatest problems, he told me that even admittedly, hostile partners can go a long way toward reducing mistrust if they will engage in frank and open dialogue.

Of course, Gorbachev is a master of the dialogue. His true optimism, backed up by his ability to analyze actual situations coolly and his faith in being able to work his way out of difficult conditions, informs all his dialogues.

Socrates (470–399 BC), one of the greatest of all dialogists, warns against falling victim to the sickness of misology (the hatred of argument or reasoning), which must be as avidly avoided as misanthropy. In a sense, to hate engaging in dialogue is to hate people. Although war and oppression often begin with their suppression, trust and love are precisely the forces that sustain and cultivate freedom of speech and dialogue, ultimately enabling them to bear precious fruit. Their innate qualities of trust and their willingness to talk, listen and allow others to talk account for the political successes achieved by both de Klerk and Gorbachev.

In the *Phaedo*, in which he discusses misology, though about to drink the cup of hemlock that will kill him, Socrates speaks with the magnanimity and courage of a philosopher certain of the immortality of the soul. True optimism of this kind does not depend on the opinions of others. Neither relative nor temporary, it is born of hope and of the individual's own resolute and unshakable convictions.

Webs of Love

IKEDA: If the collapse of fundamental national and social systems may be compared to a heart attack, the disintegration of the family, the oldest and most basic of all human institutions, may be compared to a cancer that, unnoticed in its initial stages, insidiously destroys the very substance of the body.

Saplings grow into strong trees only if they are rooted in good earth. The loving, harmonious family is the good earth of human physical and spiritual development. Its lack causes warped, twisted growth that contributes to social malaise and eventually threatens the achievement of lasting, universal peace.

Since your father was a doctor and your mother a nurse, no doubt family commitment to helping the sick and suffering exerted a positive influence on you.

GALTUNG: I agree with your estimation of the importance of the family – both the family of orientation and the family of procreation, to borrow sociologists' terminology.

Basically, the family is only as strong as the marital bond between husband and wife. If spouses discover a way of growing together so that each develops independently while both grow as a union to a level higher than would be possible for them individually, their success will permeate the whole family. My parents were successful in this respect.

Today the family is threatened from many angles. One threat is marital infidelity. The fear of AIDS certainly tends to check physical faithlessness. But this is a negative approach to the problem. Moreover, in itself total fidelity is neither a sufficient nor, probably, a necessary condition for success in marriage.

The ultimately important thing is for both partners to decide resolutely to make the marriage work by allowing love to permeate their beings and their mental attitudes to the extent that they are open to each other for the sake of mutual assistance and growth. Honesty, communication and dialogue are called for. The tremendous challenge involved in achieving such openness reminds us that love is not merely a promise or an entitlement. To bear fruit, it must be created and recreated over and over. That is the only way to solve the many problems we all encounter in marriage.

Of course, one of the most important fruits of a marriage is children. Children should be raised to be both curious and compassionate. Their basic orientations must evolve from their own inner struggles, not from indoctrination, which occurs in numerous guises. National culture is a form of indoctrination. Children should learn that there are many cultures other than the one into which they were born and should become familiar with several cultures.

The simplest and the supreme message is love. We must discover and encourage the positive in children. Mistakes should be pointed out but not dwelt on. Reward should take precedence over punishment. We must love not in order to be loved but in order to enable children to feel lovable and to love their own children when the time comes. In this way we can create threads of love to be woven into webs of love running throughout history. Perhaps this is the way to counteract the horrible brutality – usually perpetrated by males – that is the hidden truth behind many contemporary marriages. Perhaps the family in general and marriage in particular are tests we must pass in order to contribute to peace in the larger setting of world society.

IKEDA: Most human beings are closer to their families than to anyone else. According to Buddhist teachings, even cruel villains love their own wives and children. Love of family is the emotional basis on which is cultivated love of compatriots and humanity in general. Your 'webs of love' extending from generation to generation in time and from the family throughout the whole world in space are a fundamental necessity for the creation of lasting global peace.

Family life is the origin of all social activities. Goethe said that, king or peasant, the person who finds peace in the home knows supreme happiness. Or, as is set forth in the Chinese classic known as *Mojing*, the cosmos is made up of four directions – east, west, south and north – with 'home' in the center. In this age of spiritual devastation, we would do well to begin reevaluating our situation by examining family life.

As you say, children are the most important product of marital and family life. And they deserve honest, not condescending, treatment. When dealing with them – which I try to do as often as my busy schedule permits – I always think of children as individuals with personalities on a par with my own. As you know, the Japanese language makes use of various courtesy levels in speech according to the relative social positions of the parties to a conversation. Out of respect for the independence I hope they will develop, I always use courteous speech in talking with children. Taking into consideration the budding adult within each of them, I consistently try to adjust my viewpoint to theirs. Children react better when being treated as equals. Perhaps the child squatting on the department-store floor and howling for his father to buy a toy would calm down fast if the father abandoned his lofty, adult, scowling stance and joined the child on the floor.

Adults should make every effort to see the world from the child's viewpoint; it can look very different. For example, a primary-school teacher, gazing rapturously out of the clear upper panes of a classroom window, urges her young charges to rejoice at their good fortune in being able to study in a room with a wonderful view of Mount Fuji. Her effusion earns only boisterous derision from the children because the lower window panes, through which they must look, are of frosted glass.

Straight to the Heart

IKEDA: Because of such works as *A Doll's House*, Henrik Ibsen is widely regarded as a pioneer in the movement to liberate women from restricted traditional roles. In Norway, with its deep-rooted belief in the equality of the sexes, women and men now usually have equal social and political roles.

Their natural role as mothers makes women especially well suited to protecting the environment and establishing global peace. Significantly, as chair of the United Nations World Committee on the Environment and Development, Gro Harlem Brundtland – who became Norwegian prime minister in 1987 – compiled a fine and now well-known report summarizing environmental destruction. Women's contributions to these fields are likely to grow in scope and meaning in the years to come.

GALTUNG: In speaking of *A Doll's House*, you bring up another Ibsen play that I love. Originally, from the standpoint of the reader or audience member – especially its males – Ibsen appeared intolerably guilty in allowing Nora to disappear, leaving the future open as she closes the door behind her. The past is shut out; but the future – though concealed from the audience and Nora's husband, Helmer – is open. A great threat is inherent in Nora's freedom.

We can clearly imagine what a Nora of our own day would do after leaving Helmer: she would join the peace movement, the environmental movement, the development movement and – above all – the women's movement. In these activities, she would get along better without the Helmer of the play. But instead of abandoning their men as Ibsen's Nora does, today's Noras try to educate them.

The release of feminine forces long subjugated by the patriarchal system is a boon to a humankind thirsting for peace, a better environment and greater human development. Women made tremendous positive contributions to the peace movement of the 1980s. They were everywhere. Between 1981 and 1985, in addition to university lectures, I delivered about 500 addresses for peace – approximately one every three days – in twelve European countries (East and West), the United States and Japan. Most of the audiences were made up largely of women. In dialogues, their ability to transcend limited themes – for example, missile enumerations – and to think in human and holistic terms was an indispensable asset. Nonhuman, atomistic, male logic alone could never have brought about the events of 1989.

Women go straight to the heart of human suffering and happiness. Without being trapped by mental abstractions and the social hierarchies they often reflect, women think and feel in a more Buddhist way. Such thinking colors their pacifist activities. Men like to behave in the way of prospective foreign ministers, United Nations secretary-generals, or at least advisers whispering either belligerent or pacific advice in the ears of the princes of this world. Women are much less attracted to and have much less respect for such positions. Typically they establish people-to-people diplomacy and do the principal work themselves – of course, with the cooperation of many men. I do not think it strange that women are often disinclined to become parts of male-dominated hierarchies such as ministries of defense and foreign affairs. By not wasting their time in such spiritual deserts, women are able to work miracles.

The situation is similar with women's studies, the more intellectual aspect of the women's movement. Close to peace research, feminist research challenges the structural violence of the patriarchal system, the direct male violence (at least 95 per cent of all direct violence is committed by men) and the cultural violence that legitimizes the other two by simultaneously considering males superior (in that they are free to act as they like) and inferior to women (in that they are less capable of controlling their animal passions).

I do not agree with feminists who insist that patriarchy is the root of all human and social evil. Theirs is a vulgar brand of feminism that, like vulgar brands of Marxism, focuses on only one fault-line in our social construction. Gender is not everything. Other divisions play their roles: humanity in relation to nature, generation, race, class, nationality, relations with the state and with superstates, and so on. All these are important factors that resist reduction to any single common element. As Daoists warn, reductionism is dangerous. Fault-lines and yin–yang dialectics exist everywhere.

Feminist theories, like pacifist theories, introduce oriental thinking to an occident badly in need of it. Many of the basic thought-figures that Westerners – feminists and pacifists – regard as their own original discoveries are actually oriental commonplaces: yin–yang instead of Aristotelian-Cartesian or even Manichaean rigid dichotomies; process instead of structure; change instead of stasis; and lack of watertight distinctions between the normative and the descriptive, between ought to be and is. Understanding such things seems to come more easily to women than to men.

My own development took a long time and, so far, has required the struggle of writing four books on methodology and epistemology – from my *Theories and Methods of Social Research* in 1967, to my *Methodology and Development* in 1988. I had a great distance to cover. I started out as a mathematician – a delightful pursuit with an Aristotelian abhorrence of contradictions. But after about 25 years, I arrived at one basic insight: social reality is too complex and contradictory to be mirrored adequately by a non-contradictory system of thought, such as mathematics. There is a contradiction between the contradictory and the contradiction-free.

I usually find that women and orientals think more subtly about peace than men and occidentals. Fortunately, however, the latter two groups are not irredeemable.

IKEDA: Your penetrating comments on the relation between *A Doll's House* and contemporary society remind me that many writers all over the world have used Nora's experiences as a point of departure for wider social analyses. The celebrated Chinese writer Lu Xun (1881–1936) once lectured on the topic 'What happened after Nora left home?' My own mentor, Josei Toda, used Ibsen's play as study material in a series of discussions of women's liberation. He insisted that men must be more than physically strong and must strive to avoid overbearing behavior.

Men generally tend to stress the theoretical and the abstract and to lapse into exclusivist thought-systems. Intuitively, women are better at directly comprehending the essence of matters. You mention atomistic male logic and warn against the reductionist 'vulgar feminism' that blames patriarchal society for all social ills. I agree. Interpreting the diversity of actual society on the basis of any single philosophical system is dangerous. We can only improve systems and organizations after we have revolutionized our way of thinking.

Not long ago, I published a dialogue with the noted astronomer Chandra Wickramasinghe. The world-famous British astronomer Professor Fred Hoyle, whose favorite student Professor Wickramasinghe was, contributed a preface, in which he discussed the limits of reductionist science by means of a metaphor of open and closed boxes. He compared the science that has evolved against a Christian background to a closed box subject to various cultural and religious limitations. Within its limitations, it is capable of solving simple problems. Professor Hoyle says the time has come for us to adopt an open-box approach posited on the idea of relations between Earth and the whole universe. He stresses the importance of an open mind that strives for direct approaches to universal truth. To borrow Professor Hoyle's terms, men adopt a closed-box system of specific doctrines and concepts. In contrast, women are not bound to ready-made ideas and have the power of seeing the whole picture in a freer, more open fashion.

Abstract theories and concepts comprehend only parts of reality. Nonetheless, men often try to use them to alter its entirety. In their best manifestations, such attempts may be called idealistic. In their most insensitive and insidious forms, they can lead to the horror of war.

In addition to being attracted by abstract concepts, the human male is much more easily dazzled by the false idols of social position and class than is the female. Ashuras are demonlike creatures –

borrowed by Buddhism from Brahmanism – who are by nature fond of belligerence. They are described as being 84,000 *yojana* (an ancient Indian unit of linear measure variously given as 160, 120 or 64 kilometers) in height, or so tall that the waters of the oceans reach only to their knees. These proud, domineering egomaniacs are consumed by the desire to dominate everything and everyone. In this sense, they represent the worst of the male principle. In contrast to the Ashura-like male, the female tends to be gentler and more practical and to envision everything from the viewpoint of the needs of life.

Overcoming the conceptualism, exclusivism and authoritarianism of male-dominated society demands a peace movement rooted in a practical, what I like to call a life-size, approach to reality. 'Life-size' means free of abstract theories and ideas of transcendent beings – such as the Christian God – and informed by faithfulness to the best human emotions.

As you suggest, this approach is closer to the oriental way of thinking and is more compatible with the feminine way of thought. This is why I am confident that the role of women in the peace movement will grow in brilliance and importance as the years go by.

CHAPTER 2

History Persists

Citizens of the World

IKEDA: No doubt the many places you have visited in your extensive travels have made different impressions on you.

GALTUNG: Well, I guess I have been to most countries, but after having been to about 120, I stopped counting. For good or bad, all nations are expressions of human behavior. Some nationalisms are healthy; some are pathological. Some – especially the ones that consider themselves chosen by a god or by history – like to dictate behavior to and force their will on others and are therefore destructive. I like such nations less. I am much more deeply impressed by nations such as Switzerland, Canada, and maybe Finland, Costa Rica, Uruguay, the Sami and the Inuit in the Arctic, and some of the peoples of Africa such as the Masai of Kenya and the Ashanti of what is now southern Ghana, though the pasts of these last are by no means unambiguous. I am impressed by China for being less expansionist than it might have been and by Japan for having survived next to a large, powerful neighbor. Living close to very powerful neighbors, Finland and Canada are similar survivors.

As a peace researcher, I am most interested in the ways in which nations relate to other nations, not only in terms of aggression but also in terms of being able to withstand pressures from mighty neighbors. In addition, I try to discover how states contribute positively – through ideas, initiatives and sometimes money – to a peaceful world community.

If I must single out one country as the most impressive, it would have to be Switzerland. In spite of its dubious banking industry, Switzerland, which is linguistically four nations and religiously two, deserves great respect for cohesiveness. Further, in spite of a certain macho militarism, the Swiss posture of nonprovocative self-defense capability is very appealing.

Having begun as a confederation* – the Swiss Confederation or Confederatio Helvetica, named for the ancient Helvetians, is still

---

* Confederation (German: *Staatenbund*): an interstate organization (with several citizenships), with member states cooperating in all fields, but independent, free to leave.

29

the official name of the country – Switzerland today is more a federation*. This alteration in its structure may prove its undoing if it becomes something more like a unitary state, a system that has imprisoned many nations. Such constructions do not survive; neither do multinational federations, as the recent histories of the Soviet Union, Yugoslavia and Czechoslovakia illustrate. But because of the great inspiration and hope still surviving there, I have lived in or near Switzerland for much of the past 25 years.

IKEDA: Like you, I consider myself a citizen of the world and, by traveling and working for the sake of peace for all peoples everywhere, try to be worthy of the title. In 1975, on the occasion of the First Soka Gakkai International World Peace Conference, held on the island of Guam, we all signed an official register. In the citizenship column beside my name, I wrote: 'the World'. I have undertaken travels to Asia, the Middle East, Europe, the Soviet Union, and North, Central and South America, not for the sake of any single nation or religion, but because I consider it my duty and mission as a Buddhist.

Great people always transcend national boundaries and ethnic differences to arouse sympathy in the hearts of people all over the globe. As is well known, Socrates called himself a citizen not of Athens, but of the world. His pupil Plato (427–347 BC), too, was a citizen of the world. The American poet and philosopher Ralph Waldo Emerson (1803–82) said that Plato, though a Greek, belonged to no specific village and no specific nation. The English reader sees something very English in Plato, the German reader finds him Germanic, while the Italian finds him Roman as well as Greek. Everyone who beheld her extraordinary beauty felt kinship with Helen of Troy. So Plato's great humanity awakens a sense of intimate closeness with all people who read him, no matter what their race or nation.

You speak most favorably of Switzerland. My own four visits to that country remain indelibly imprinted on my memory because of the warm sincerity with which the local people welcomed me. Albert Einstein, too, was very fond of Switzerland. He completed high school and technical college there and, at the age of 22, became a Swiss citizen. He is said to have proudly cherished both the natural beauty of the country and the warm humanity of its citizens.

The famous educator Johann Heinrich Pestalozzi (1746–1827) – of whom I wrote a biography for young Japanese readers when

---

* Federation (German: *Bundesstaat*): an intra-state organization (with one citizenship), where the parts are sovereign in internal affairs, but have joint financial, foreign, military and police policies.

I myself was a younger man – was Swiss but considered himself a product of the world and of all humanity. For this reason he felt he would be at home anywhere fate saw fit to put him. Switzerland provides a model of harmony and cooperation precisely because of the inspiration and hope that, as you point out, survive there.

GALTUNG: Does your designation of yourself as a citizen of the world arise from the philosophy of Mahayana Buddhism? I assume that for you as a Buddhist, a citizen of the world is unrestrained by nation-state structures and racial discrimination.

IKEDA: Yes. The kind of person whom ancient Indian philosophers described as a person of 'all four directions' acts as a true cosmopolitan, indifferent to racial or national categories. This approach arises naturally from views of humanity and the universe based on the Buddhist doctrine of dependent origination (a fundamental Buddhist teaching that all things exist because of their relations with other things). Nichiren Daishonin, who considered national authorities insignificant, disdained the rulers of Japan as no more than the proprietors of a small island country.

A citizen of the world whose spiritual life is founded on Mahayana Buddhism is unaffected by narrow racialism. The Mahayana doctrines of the absence of a persisting self and of dependent origination – both major teachings – cultivate a cosmopolitan approach in the Buddhist citizen of the world.

All phenomena in the universe, including the self, come into and go out of being as a consequence of mutual dependence (*engi** in Japanese). Advocates of this philosophy do not allow themselves to be obsessed by exclusive possession of material things, or by the supposed special excellence of any given class, race or nation. A true Buddhist transcends individual, racial and national egoism. Realizing that all things are connected and interlinked, the Buddhist disregards discriminatory barriers.

Buddhism strives to create a world characterized by understanding of dependent origination and by the essential nature of all things as latent potentiality (*shunyata* in Sanskrit, or *ku* in Japanese). In terms of human society, this means a world of mutual assistance and support, a world in which all people respect all others as being endowed with fundamentally important missions. In such a world of altruistic compassion, all-pervasive mutual rela-

---

Engi: Dependent origination. Also dependent causation, conditioned co-arising or co-production. A fundamental Buddhist doctrine of the interdependence of things. It teaches that all beings and phenomena exist or occur only because of their relationship with other beings or phenomena. Therefore, nothing can exist in absolute independence of other things or arise of its own accord. (From *A Dictionary of Buddhist Terms and Concepts*, Nichiren Shoshu International Center, Tokyo, 1983).

tionships mean that working for the happiness of the other person is tantamount to working for one's own happiness.

Going beyond interpersonal human relations, the wisdom of the teachings of dependent origination and universal latent potentiality extends to relations between human and nonhuman nature everywhere. Enlightenment to this wisdom gives birth to a sense of the solidarity of all things as emanations of universal life. This in turn inspires trust, compassion and nonviolence and eliminates violence, war and economic destruction, which work to sever the threads of solidarity in universal life.

Thus the sense of being a citizen of the world, member of humanity and an integral part of universal life arises naturally from Buddhist teachings of dependent origination and latent potentiality – that is, *engi* and *ku*.

Article 9

IKEDA: To a great extent, Japan's economic recovery and growth after World War II can be attributed to our unique constitution – the Peace Constitution, so called because of its famous Article 9, which rejects belligerence as a means of dealing with international disagreements. In recent years, however, the very basis of the document has been called into question.

GALTUNG: The famous Article 9 of the Japanese constitution is open to various interpretations. It may be regarded as totally pacifist, a rejection not only of war but also of the instruments of war; that is, of the military, even of a self-defense force. It may also be viewed as having been imposed on Japan by the victors in World War II and therefore something to be repudiated at the right time. Such an interpretation opens the way for 'normalization', which today, unfortunately, means maintaining a military organization with offensive capabilities. Still another interpretation would lie between these two extremes. My own views tend in that direction.

I regard the Peace Constitution as an asset, not a liability, for Japan. If I were a Japanese politician, I would reason in the following way. Although not alone in doing so, my country was guilty of evil during the war in the Pacific. While including a punitive element, the constitution challenges Japan to use Article 9 creatively. I would therefore make a distinction between a military organization with offensive capability – ruled out by Article 9 – and a purely defensive force (as described in my book *There Are Alternatives!*). In addition, I would indicate willingness to participate in the United Nations forces, but only in the sense of peacekeeping (Chapter 6 of the United Nations Charter), not in peace-enforcement (Chapter 7) forces. As was demonstrated by the Gulf War, peace enforcement involves waging actual war 'with all necessary means', perhaps killing hundreds of thousands of people. This ought not to be the task of the United Nations, and certainly violates Article 9 of the Japanese constitution.

Peacekeeping operations stipulated under Chapter 6 of the charter already have a long and respected history. Insofar as doing so requires only hand weapons and, ideally, nonviolent techniques and conflict-mediating skills, Japan should take part in efforts to police the many agreements and settlements we shall require in the years to come.

Ultimately, the historical significance of the Peace Constitution is to be found in its redefinition of the military. Gone are the days when a country might attack another for nothing but its own advantage. Gone, too, are the times when countries could be permitted to intervene in other nations' affairs for their own interests or to oppose regimes not to their liking. Military organizations can no longer be legitimately used to attack other social classes. We now need a world where countries maintain purely defensive forces and participate in peacekeeping operations agreed upon by the global community. In other words, the task is not to abolish the military but to redefine its role, making it part of a peaceful community of nations. If I were a Japanese politician, I would be proud that my country is the first to commit itself to this very significant task. Instead of abolishing Article 9, the Japanese people should recommend that other states, for instance the United States, the country that more than any other has intervened militarily abroad, include similar provisions in their own constitutions.

IKEDA: During the war in the Persian Gulf, hectic debates raged over whether Japan should remain devoted solely to peace or should fulfill what many regard as our international obligations by taking part in the operations. Deliberations on this dilemma gave rise to the idea of reviewing the previously sacrosanct constitution. I welcome free debate on the issue. But the outcome at the time was only further aggravation of a situation in which we are compelled to make a decision between two alternatives: preserving the constitution as it is or revising it. People found it hard to imagine yet another alternative on a higher level; that is, an alternative of the kind you propose.

Your stimulating idea of reinterpreting the constitution, only insofar as viewing it as permission to cooperate in United Nations peacekeeping actions, offers valuable hints in connection with the still continuing debates on this topic. Certainly, cooperation with the United Nations is essential.

At the same time, self-discipline is absolutely indispensable if we are to make optimum use of our devotion to lasting peace. As you know, many Asian nations, where memories of past Japanese militarist atrocities remain fresh, regarded Japan's military participation in United Nations peacekeeping operations in Cambodia in the early 1990s with misgivings. To calm such misgivings, while making the most energetic international contributions, Japan must remain a model of self-discipline at home and abroad.

You have gone so far as to recommend amending the constitution of the United States to include a disavowal of the right to belligerency like the one stated in Article 9 of the Japanese constitution. I agree with you. The constitution of Japan bases security policies not on armed might, but on international amity created by mutual trust. The Japanese legal break with past belligerent traditions represented by this article is very significant.

Conflict between the Eastern and Western blocs has ended. A new world order is needed. I am convinced that we must make the spirit of the Japanese Peace Constitution and that of the United Nations Charter cornerstones of that new order. To achieve this end, an upsurge of antiwar world public opinion must be stimulated; and all nations must be urged to adopt constitutional measures rejecting the right of belligerency.

GALTUNG: In my book *Japan in the World Community* (published in Japanese in 1988), I adopt the position that Article 9 of the Japanese constitution does not exclude what I consider the acceptable functions of the military; that is, purely defensive activities based only on territory and United Nations peacekeeping (not peace-enforcing) operations. Such undertakings as acting as international police or providing emergency control and aid in time of catastrophe are badly needed. In spite of some leftist (in the bad sense of the word) antimilitary sentiment, public opinion in general supports operations of these kinds. A pacifist and a conscientious objector myself, I oppose discrimination against people in military uniform. The important thing is what military people do, not the kind of clothes they wear. They must be resisted when they attack other countries, open fire on the working class or overthrow legitimate regimes. But not if they carry out the functions mentioned above.

The list of positive military functions can be extended. Nearly 30, mostly very small, countries in the world today lack armies. Should war occur in their vicinities, big powers are likely to invite themselves to act as the small countries' protectors. It would be better to station, at their invitation, preemptive United Nations peacekeeping forces in small countries to guard against untoward occurrences. Like the police in most nations, such forces would perform a deterrent role merely by being on the scene. Permanently installing peacekeeping forces might influence public opinion more than verbal appeals and could lead to the gradual internationalization and softening of military power. Instead of trying to become another military power, Japan should actively promote such courses of development, thus encouraging a positive interpretation of Article 9 of the Japanese constitution.

A Pacific Civilization

IKEDA: Economic performance in Asia and on the Pacific periphery has attracted great attention and generated hopes for the emergence of the latent powers of the entire region. I, however, have long been more interested in this part of the world in relation to the further evolution of civilization on a broader scale than economics alone.

When I spoke with him 20 years ago, Dr Richard Coudenhove-Kalergi, the so-called father of the European Community, now called the European Union, said to me, 'We are in a transitional period, moving gradually from the Atlantic civilization of Europe and America to a Pacific civilization … Japan will become a mainstay of the coming Pacific civilization.' Similarly, on the basis of his own views of history, the celebrated English historian Arnold J. Toynbee (1889–1975), with whom I was privileged to carry on an extended, intimate dialogue, foresaw the emergence of a Pacific civilization.

Of course, at present the region is unsettled. The major issue now is to discover the best ways to use its latent potentials for the sake of humanity in general. To build a Pacific civilization that is both peaceful and open, we must avoid over-reliance on political, military and economic elements and must incorporate the spiritual wisdom of the East in our approach.

GALTUNG: I direct the small Pacific Hemisphere Project (PHP) from the University of Hawaii, where I spend each spring session. Yet I think in terms not of a homogeneous Pacific culture, but of a Pacific civilization encompassing many cultures in an open and tolerant way, much as the culture of the state of Hawaii itself embraces diverse cultural elements.

In Hawaii, the ordinary people, often on religious grounds, organize many activities that facilitate cross-cultural enjoyment and enrichment. The only serpents in the Hawaiian paradise are the people who insist on the superiority of a particular culture, for which they demand a position of primacy, priority and predominance.

During its militaristic period (say from 1931 to 1945), the Japanese attempted to force their language and culture on many other peoples and failed. The United States has been trying the same thing for a long time, though in a slightly subtler way. Instead of forcing people to give up their vernaculars to replace them with English, Americans reward other people for becoming what they call 'good Americans'. But they, too, are doomed to fail. Though they may seem downtrodden – as the Hawaiians, Australian Aborigines and the Ainus of Japan sometimes do – all cultures are strong and resilient. Judaism survived even Hitler.

The Pacific region requires cooperatively run institutions that are not dominated by any specific country or group of countries trying to bully all the others. Preferably the memberships of such institutions should include representatives from the eastern rim of the ocean (North, Central and South America); the western rim (Russia, Japan, a united Korea, a united China, the former Indochina, the nations of ASEAN); the center (meaning the Pacific Islands); Australia and New Zealand; both the Arctic and Antarctic regions; and all indigenous people throughout the zone. This means an immense cultural richness. Taking the place of militarism, a pan-Pacific community organized as a confederation would rectify many of the evils that now afflict the hemisphere and would be the best way of preventing a second tragedy, or second Pacific war. Of course, a major confrontation between the United States and Japan would be devastating to all.

IKEDA: In October 1992, in a lecture entitled 'The Twenty-first Century and East Asian Civilization', which I delivered on the occasion of being made an honorary research professor at the Chinese Academy of Social Sciences, I cited the ethos of symbiosis as the source of that civilization. By this I meant 'a psychological tendency to favor harmony over opposition, unity over division, "we" over "I"; a belief that human beings should live together harmoniously with each other and with nature, support each other and flourish together'. It seems to me that all of these characteristics will be essential to global civilization in the next century. I am convinced that the idea of *symbiosis* will help humanity move in new directions.

Your idea of a pan-Pacific community is profoundly linked to what I call the ethos of symbiosis. In periods of prosperity and decline, Western civilization has shifted its center from the Mediterranean to the Atlantic and then to the shores of the Pacific. I am not thinking in terms of such shifts. Instead, I envision diverse cultures coexisting in a symbiotic state of mutual respect. I hope such a community can become symbolic of the twenty-first century.

Achieving this aim will require harmony within what you term 'immense cultural richness'. How to achieve this harmony remains an unknown. But I am convinced that it will require us to abandon our past habit of thinking inductively and switch to deductive thinking.

Among the growing number of Western intellectuals attempting to see their own civilization in a relative light, the leading French Sinologist Leon Vandermeersch occupies a prominent position. In my speech to the China Academy of Social Sciences, I made use of his words when I said:

> The remarks in this regard by the authoritative French Sinologist Professor Leon Vandermeersch are rich in significance: 'Confucianism could not but disappear with the old society … But precisely when Confucianism is completely dead can its legacy begin to be reinvested in new forms of thought without conflicting with the various factors of development.' The re-investment of Confucianism's legacy alluded to here could help us find an antidote to the excessive individualism of Western civilization and guide us toward universal value in the 'Way of Humanity'. That will be mutually stimulating, a product of this reinvestment of the Confucian legacy. The attainment of these goals is a major task for twenty-first century civilization.

I agree with you that large-scale confrontation between the United States and Japan must be averted. In a speech I delivered at Harvard University (September 26, 1991), I said that we must never again follow the course that led to Pearl Harbor. To avoid this, we must realize the importance of what I call 'soft power'; that is, all kinds of exchanges and contacts on nongovernmental levels. For the sake of the future, we must not allow relations between the United States and Japan to be confined to governmental contacts. This is why Soka Gakkai International works enthusiastically to build a network of peace and mutual trust at the grassroots level. For the sake of global symbiosis, exchanges among ordinary people are far more effective than contacts between governments.

Masterful Communicators

IKEDA: In addition to Mikhail Gorbachev, among the leaders of the earth-shaking developments in Eastern Europe, I am especially interested in Vaclav Havel, who led Czechoslovakia through what has come to be called the Velvet Revolution. Both Mr Gorbachev and Mr Havel are masterful communicators. In a conversation with me, Mr Gorbachev frequently demonstrated his own faith in communications with comments such as: 'People laughed when I proposed constructing a world without nuclear weapons and employing dialogue rather than violence to settle disputes. But, as you can see yourself, these aims are now becoming realities.'

The texts of Mr Havel's speeches reveal the playwright's keen sensitivity to language, which he uses appropriately yet cautiously. Patently, he, too, believes in the importance to political leadership of dialogue and the accurate use of language. I suggest that the emphasis both men put on verbal communication contributes to the freshness of their approaches. As philosopher-statesmen, they are models for the emulation of future political leaders. The effectiveness of speech and dialogue must not be overlooked.

GALTUNG: The so-called Velvet Revolution – if any revolution of the kind ever took place – came to Czechoslovakia as a gift from East Germany, one of the countries the people of Czechoslovakia liked least. Friends have told me that a maximum of 2,400 people participated in the Velvet Revolution. In East Germany, on the other hand, great segments of the population rebelled. Some adopted the venerable nonviolent technique of mass migration, to West Germany via Hungary. Others – notably in Leipzig on 9 October 1989 – confronted the well-armed Stasi, face to face, on the streets, nonviolently.

Perhaps because of the contrast between the situations in East Germany and Czechoslovakia, I am less impressed by Havel's words than some are. Still, needing a hero, the people of Czechoslovakia created one. In 1968, their then leader, Alexander Dubček (1921–90), acted more courageously and against greater odds. In a sense, long before Polish Solidarity, Dubček set in motion a train of events that have only recently reached their culmination. In this, he resembles Nikita Khrushchev (1894–1971), who, in his way, had already rebelled against Stalinism in February 1956.

Verbal expression is of course very important. And, for a person who must communicate and engage in dialogues frequently, certain conclusions about them take shape.

Ideally, communication should be two-way. I find television and radio performances very unsatisfactory. Books, too, are a one-way communication. Of course, the writing of books helps authors develop their own ways of thinking, and written texts may trigger autonomous thought-processes in readers. Although I do not disregard the value of teleconferences, there is no substitute for direct, face-to-face dialogue.

I often find that I communicate best by avoiding a direct approach and by employing such powerful communications devices as images, visions, models and metaphors. One system of metaphors that I have recently used extensively is the comparison between peace and health.

Repression and exploitation are the two most basic modern forms of structural violence; cardiovascular diseases and cancer are the two basic somatic conditions brought on by modernization. Repression and cardiovascular diseases are similar in that both impede circulation. Exploitation and cancer resemble each other in that a part of the social or human organism lives at the expense of the rest. Peace research and health research are metaphors for each other; each can learn from the other. Similarly, both peace theory and medical science emphasize the role of consciousness and mobilization in healing.

Humor is another important aspect of verbal communication. Contemplation of the meaning of peace in the form of reduction and possible elimination of violence confronts us with many horrors and with rampant violence and suffering. We cannot overlook these things. We must confront them, because we must understand what we are up against in the family, the community and the world. At the same time, we must learn to live with them. Encapsulating our insights in ways that invite smiles, or even laughter, is one way of living with them. Obviously suffering and violence are not joking matters to be laughed away. Still, whereas the brain may be less readily accessible, the heart can be reached with smiles – including smiles at ourselves and our own frequent clownish folly. The smile can improve possibilities for dialogue. Further, it can elicit in us compassion for the victims of violence instead of allowing us to remain cut off from their suffering.

I see the dialogue as almost the opposite of the debate. There are winners and losers in debates. One party triumphs over the opponent by catching him or her in contradictions between values and facts or on facts or values. The dialogue, however, is open-ended. Participating in a dialogue in which the outcome is known from the start is a waste of time. Dialogues must promote mutual enrichment; in them there can be only winners. Both parties lay all their cards – their insights – on the table, holding nothing back to trump with later. Like love, the dialogue is generous. It can be beautiful. I am always grateful not only to my fellow participants in dialogues, but also to the dialogue itself as a human possibility. As the British, who do this kind of thing very well, might say, a dialogue is a 'good conversation' in the old, bourgeois sense.

IKEDA: Perhaps you have the ancient Sophists in mind when you make a sharp distinction between the dialogue and the debate. Of course, it is impossible to condone the Sophist fashion of employing rhetorical skill to demonstrate that something is what it is not; for instance, that black is white.

Like you, by dialogue I mean mutually enriching, free and open discussion. A true dialogue must be a candid, sincere engagement. There is no place in it for condescension or false familiarity. Dialogues are most productive when they are incandescent, person-to-person exchanges of opinion. Although they have value of their own, debates involving large numbers of people are less useful. As the French philosopher Henri Bergson (1859–1941) once said, discussion among more than 25 people is fruitless. The more numerous the participants, the less likely are the exchanges to be sincere. In such cases, speakers tend increasingly to concentrate on getting the better of their co-debaters by demonstrating the kind of hunger for domination characteristic of the ancient Sophists. Bergson felt it is impossible to put any trust at all in such confrontations.

At their best, dialogues are unaffected encounters between two total personalities. This is why, as you say, they are much more stimulating and enriching than one-way communications like reading or radio and television performances. According to Goethe, writing is an abuse of words and silent reading only a wretched substitute for living dialogue. He believed that the human being conveys possibilities directly to another human being only by means of his or her individuality.

Agreeing with this assessment, I consider dialogue one of the noblest and most important acts in which human beings can participate. I have taken part in as many as possible in the past and, on the basis of my firm belief in their value, am resolved to continue doing so for the rest of my life.

The Floodgate of Free Expression

IKEDA: Unfortunately, much of the trial-and-error process of perestroika that Mikhail S. Gorbachev put into motion has been mercilessly frustrated. Nonetheless, the policy of freedom of speech or openness, glasnost, remains one of his shining achievements and I believe is related to the very innermost character of the man himself. Trust among human beings is restored when opinions can be freely exchanged in written and spoken form.

No such trust and no such freedom of expression existed in the pre-Gorbachev Kremlin, which was a chilling den of mistrust, darkness and fear. It was too oppressed by doctrines of power, authority, militarism and violence to permit open discussion on any topic. Most of the people working there merely postured for political ends.

But Gorbachev's emphasis on dialogue opened the floodgates through which the long-constrained emotions of the Soviet peoples found abundant expression. With glasnost, the word – printed and spoken – gradually began manifesting its essential power. No longer afraid of the authorities, people started expressing their true opinions so freely indeed that long-winded debates have replaced the stifled silence of the past.

I have held five discussions with Mr Gorbachev: two while he was still president, one in April 1992, another in April 1993 and still another in May 1994. On all these occasions, he impressed me as a man who knows how to talk and who hears and heeds what others say.

GALTUNG: I fully share your high regard for Mikhail Sergeyevich Gorbachev, an historical personage and one of the necessary conditions for the ending of the Cold War. (In my opinion, the other two were the dissident movement in the East and the peace movements in the East and the West.) Gorbachev's lack of popularity in Russia may stem from several causes. One is simple: he is held responsible for the implosion of the Soviet empire. In addition, perhaps he was too big for his country; there may be some truth after all in the notion that a prophet is without honor in his own land. Or perhaps people were displeased by his failure to make a 180-degree about-face, like many others who were disgusted with the post-Stalinist situation. Gorbachev wanted both market principles and guarantees against social misery. He wanted to loosen but not break up the Soviet Union. His thinking was too complex for the popular demand to turn from the secular god of planning to the secular god of the market – from one monotheism to another – instead of trying for polytheism or pantheism. But when the people have seen enough of the madness of undiluted periphery and command capitalism – and that is surely what they are going to get – Gorbachev's time may come again.

Like you, I greatly appreciate the value of dialogue. To indicate how greatly, I might cite the following story. In September 1968 I was invited by the regime of the German Democratic Republic – East Germany – to attend a forum in Weimar. Not unexpectedly, it transpired that the aim of the forum was to condemn US aggression in Vietnam and to recognize East Germany, which I saw as a necessary condition for orienting the Cold War confrontation in a more promising direction. As it turned out, I had been distributing information on nonmilitary defense in Vietnam in January of the same year and in Prague a few days after the brutal invasion of that city by forces of the Warsaw Pact. At the forum, I spoke first against the US war in Vietnam and then turned my attention to Czechoslovakia.

I experienced an audience reaction similar to others I have known in many places – for instance, at Princeton University when I addressed students on the genocide, structure-cide and culture-cide conducted by European settlers against Native Americans. Then, as in Weimar, everyone in the room knew I was right. But the topic was taboo. The audience cast their eyes downward. They tried to disassociate themselves from the speaker by avoiding eye-contact. They hoped the painful incident would soon end. No dialogue took place.

At Princeton, my talk ran its full course. At Weimar, however, the painful situation was dramatically and suddenly terminated. While I was speaking, two hefty, gorilla-like men in black appeared from a door in the background. As I described the invasion of Prague and my own efforts to distribute material on nonmilitary self-defense, they grabbed my legs and arms and dragged me away from the lectern. For a few moments, I was still able to address the group because I clung to the microphone, which had a long cord. But I was soon hustled out of the room and into a black car that raced to the airport, where I was to be exported like a leper.

The authorities had decided that the trouble was with me and not in the streets of Prague. For that reason, they sent a Marxist professor of theology to converse with me during my ride to the airport. This, they reasoned, was the level on which my own philo-sophical-moral problem had to be addressed.

The professor's approach was not unintelligent. He asked me, 'Which is worse: the killing of maybe a million Indochinese peasants or the practically bloodless invasion of Czechoslovakia?' I replied that, of course, the former is worse. While railing against the East, the West is guilty of much racism and hypocrisy. But this is no excuse for destroying the seeds of the freedom for which a people longs. As the saying aptly has it: 'Two wrongs don't make a right.'

I was dragged from the platform because the local regime had no tradition of glasnost, no tradition of giving voice, of uttering the offensive word or of speaking the unspeakable. Emperor-worship once created a similar situation in Japan, where each social order functioned under such strong taboos that even mentioning the taboos was taboo.

Germany, a country that I consider in many regards democratic, still labors under at least four near-taboos. One is talking in any depth about the United States, since this invariably brings up the client relationship to a country with a very violent legacy. Another is talking about Jews or Israel, for understandable reasons. The third is talking about the European Union, which has become the new German identity, the new Motherland, to the point of replacing German nationalism in the minds of many. And the final taboo is talking in any depth about Germany itself. Taken together, these reluctances amount to fairly heavy limitations on public debate. Therefore, although their taboos were more comprehensive, we must not condemn only the Stalinist and post-Stalinist countries in this respect. Nothing is more dangerous to democracy than taboos that impede free dialogue.

We must not assume that censorship only takes the form of an insignificant person wielding a red pencil in the room next to the editor's. The censor can exist in the editor's head and can be cloned into all other heads. This is why many newspapers in the

United States are boringly identical. Although the nation fortunately has some independent weeklies and monthlies, very few people read them. The book I have written with Richard Vincent, *USA Glasnost* is about precisely this topic.

Gorbachev offered his own people and the world a true dialogue and performed a seminal role in reviving Europe. Like certain animals, he was discarded after his job had been performed. We must rejoice that he was not killed.

IKEDA: Gorbachev's complex maneuverings were less his own fault than the inevitable outcome of conditions in the Soviet Union at the time. The choices he made were unavoidable for a responsible politician. Although perestroika has been a trial-and-error affair, his faith in the process of glasnost and democratization remains unshaken. By transforming both the Soviet Union and, in a real sense, the whole world, he accomplished a task to which no one before had ever been equal.

The opinions of many knowledgeable and observant people give an accurate picture of the excellence of Gorbachev's achievements. For example, in assessing him as a great personage, Aleksandr N. Yakovlev (assistant director of the Gorbachev Fund) has said that, while relinquishing the power he held in his own hands, Gorbachev saved the peoples of the whole world from fear of another global conflict. Fedor M. Burlatsky (former editor-in-chief of the newspaper *Literaturnaya Gazeta*) has remarked, 'Gorbachev is the first politician in the Soviet Union to believe in parliamentary democracy.' Vaclav Havel has observed that Gorbachev came to office a typical bureaucrat and left office a democrat.

Free discussion and violence are antipodal. Gorbachev made free speech his main weapon for two good reasons. First, he knew that perestroika could not succeed without popular support and that popular support is impossible without open discussion. Second, he realized that, though they may have temporary superficial results, enforced changes ultimately end in nothing because to be successful, changes must begin in the hearts and minds of the masses.

The people must believe in the justness of what is being done. Authority alone is not enough to ensure lasting results. The collapse of the apparently monolithic Soviet Union in very short order after the inception of perestroika indicates loss of popular faith in Communist Party rule and growing mistrust and doubt. After all, in the first free elections of deputies, Communist candidates lost in droves.

I suspect that Gorbachev himself foresaw the likelihood of his being 'discarded', to use your word. Once at the Kremlin, he said to me:

The first step in perestroika is giving the people freedom. It remains to be seen how they will use that freedom. A person long shut up in a prison or a well is blinded by the sun when suddenly brought into the open air. Similarly, in using their freedom, newly liberated people think not about the present, but about the past. Instead of concentrating on the world order, they turn their eyes only to domestic issues.

As might be expected from a politician with a philosophical bent, this remark calls to mind Plato's famous metaphor of the cave.

The noted writer Chingiz Aitmatov, whom I have already mentioned, told me of a Kremlin episode that vividly illustrates both Gorbachev's extraordinary statesmanship and his anticipations of the future. Once the two of them were discussing an oriental fable in connection with the hard choices politicians must make. In the story, as part of several prophecies made to a statesman, a certain wandering sage tells of a newly enfranchised people determined to avenge their past slavery on the politician they consider responsible for it:

In front of the crowd, they will criticize you, laugh boisterously at you, ridicule both you and your close associates, publicly abuse you and your faithful comrades and defy your orders. Until your very last day, they will revile you and trample on your name. You will be unable to escape from the ambitions of those around you. Great statesman, you are free to chose your own fate.

As Aitmatov feared, this fable proved prophetic about the fate awaiting Gorbachev himself. After listening to it and thinking silently for a moment, however, Gorbachev said:

I've made my choice. And once I've chosen my path, I will not swerve from it, no matter what sacrifice is demanded of me. My sole aim is democracy, liberty and extrication from all the despotism of the horrifying past. The people can judge me as they like … Even if many of my contemporaries fail to understand me, I am determined to follow this course.

Whether ultimately triumph or tragedy, Gorbachev's life as a statesman – which I do not consider over yet – is a source of pride for him. And though out of office at present, he is one of those rare people who participate constructively in the drama even in a diminished role.

GALTUNG: And even if he should not return, there may be other Gorbachevs on the way. Let us hope that next time his own people will not be allowed to crucify him, as the Jews did Jesus, thus allowing a Barabbas to become president. Now the West fully supports Boris Yeltsin, an *apparatchik* who never uttered a dissident word in his life, trusting that he will have no objections to the West. A bad sign indeed, for the West as well as for Russia.

Socialism: Pro and Con

IKEDA: In the light of the events of the past few years, the word 'socialism' has acquired dramatically new connotations. There is even an ironic Russian joke to the effect: 'Workers of the world – sorry!' ought to replace the admonition in the *Communist Manifesto*: 'Workers of the world, unite!' Historically speaking, we may be justified in agreeing with US statesman Zbigniew Brzezinski in labeling socialism in the fixed form of Marxist-Leninism a 'grand failure'. Nonetheless, some socialist ideas deserve respect and retention.

In its original form, socialism was an admirable attempt to assist laboring peoples relentlessly exploited by capitalism in its early, oppressive stages. Many people have found the fundamental socialist ideal of universal social equality and justice a source of moral strength. Since capitalism and liberalism might not have survived without the influence of certain socialist ideas, to refer to what happened in the Soviet Union and East Europe as the triumph of capitalism is an oversimplification.

GALTUNG: Capitalism has survived by relegating its horrors and victims to lower working classes at home and by exporting them to peripheral Third World regions. Socialism collapsed because it was honest enough to keep victims of the system at home, and not only in the lower classes. Brzezinski is correct to speak of failure, but it was Stalinism, not socialism, that failed.

Essentially Stalinism consisted of four factors. First, there was massive planning in which perhaps only 400 people planned macro-economics and even micro-economics for some 400 million people throughout the former Soviet Union and Eastern Europe. Production was on a gigantic scale with quantity achieved at the expense of quality; but grinding misery was basically eliminated. Second, the Communist Party monopolized power and even truth. Third, the civil and human rights that humanity had developed at immense cost were totally neglected. And, fourth, to all this was added a solid dose of traditional Russian imperialism in Russia, in the Soviet Union and in the former satellite countries.

This system richly deserved the collapse it suffered at the hands of the very people it was supposed to serve. In splendid, nonviolent revolutions prior to and during 1989, the people of Poland, Hungary and above all East Germany shook off that system. Ultimately others followed.

Be that as it may, US analysts, unexposed to democratic socialism and social democracy, are dishonest in attempting to claim that the cruel Stalinist system is all there is to socialism. I subscribe, as do many other people, to a group of four elements as positive aspects of a socialism based on equality and justice. First, there should be a mixed economy, or so-called negotiation economy, bringing together state and capital, planning and market, in a permanent, transparent and accessible dialogue. Of course, this presupposes a decent, well-run public sector. Second, the first priority in production must be to satisfy the basic needs of the poorest. Elimination of misery is the goal, not mathematical equality. Third, the country must retain control over all its international economic transactions. And fourth, there should be open democratic discussion of economic priorities. These highly laudable aspects of social democracy must not be discarded as a consequence of the justified general disgust with Stalinism.

IKEDA: What you say is consonant in many respects with a proposal I once made for a humane socialism. My idea is to create a social structure guided by compassion. The failings of capitalism and of the law of the jungle into which it easily lapses run counter to the spirit of compassion that is fundamental to Buddhist teachings. Some of those failings include facile acceptance of social injustice, oppression of the have-nots by the haves, and reliance on the charity of a few philanthropists to provide help for the weak.

Obviously I do not advocate the creation of a society like that of the former Soviet Union, in which a hypertrophic bureaucracy dominated all social planning. A mixed economy with substantial provisions made for the welfare of the weak is the kind of social structure needed if the ordinary masses are to preserve their vitality and enjoy equality and prosperity. I see much in common between my own vision and the points you set forth.

Georgiy K. Shakhnazarov, who served as aide to President Gorbachev, held a meeting with Zbigniew Brzezinski in 1989, at which he pointed out the mistake of lumping socialism and communism together as if they were the same and trying to bury both. He pointed to historical cases in which capitalism has overcome crises while preserving its vigor by introducing socialist elements. Instead of signaling the downfall of socialist ideals, the dramatic changes that occurred in the Soviet Union and Eastern Europe in the 1980s marked the failure of attempts to build a socialist society without democracy and the market. What collapsed in that decade was, as you say, the rigid Stalinist system of central authority and the control and exploitation of East European nations, which were forced to serve as a buffer zone for the Soviet Union. Basically Shakhnazarov and Brzezinski agreed on these points.

It is dangerous for the capitalist nations to proclaim the downfall of socialism for no more than reasons of political publicity. Doing so deprives them of a mirror in which to observe their own faults. The important thing is not which social system won or lost but human happiness and the quality of life. Social systems are only expedients for providing ordinary people with the means to live well.

Gorbachev's perestroika inspired repulsion against sacrificing the masses in the name of central authority. Sooner or later, the people always bring about the destruction of a social structure that ignores them. For this reason, I think capitalist nations ought to find abundant food for self-reflection in the downfall of the Soviet Union.

Perestroika

IKEDA: In content, scope and influence, Mikhail Gorbachev's policy of perestroika constituted a revolution. Former British Prime Minister Margaret Thatcher was correct in saying that the events of 1917 were minor in comparison with it. Communist history has been marred by far too much bloodshed. Perestroika was a great experiment for humanity because it accomplished a largely bloodless revolution.

GALTUNG: A few years ago, nearly 300 million people lived in the Soviet Union, the largest country on Earth. Realizing that his nation was a theater of the absurd, traveling down a track to nowhere, the political genius Mikhail Gorbachev wanted to change the script by calling the bluff of the leaders of the old system. He certainly called their bluff, but he may have overlooked one or two important points.

People accustomed to being led by propaganda of one kind or another for centuries – maybe even a millennium – easily fall prey to a new propaganda when an old one is discredited. Gorbachev wanted something economically midway between capitalism and socialism and a political structure intermediary between a con-federation and a federation.

But, laboring under the Bogomil* curse of absolutism, their equivalent of Manichaeism, the Russians believe in clear-cut dichotomies, not in middle paths. For them capitalism was the only possible alternative to communism. And the only alternative to the Soviet Union was dis-union; that is, full independence for all the republics and the formation of a Commonwealth of Independent

---

* Bogomil: A dualist sect founded in Bulgaria in the medieval period that advocated the idea that God had two sons: the good son Christ and the evil son Satan.

States, which exists mainly on paper. Washington replaced Moscow as the center of the world, and the Russians started paying attention to practically no one but the Americans.

Gorbachev proposed much broader, complex solutions to the Soviet dilemma. I think his way was better because it was more realistic. But he appealed primarily to the brains of perhaps 10 per cent of the population, instead of talking to the hearts of the nearly 300 million people who held him responsible for the demise of the system they knew. Such people were uninterested in the alternatives he proposed. If a socialist Soviet Union was no longer feasible, they wanted its opposite.

The drama continues. The peoples of the former Soviet Union will soon come to see what capitalism means for peripheral areas when they themselves become such peripheral zones of global capitalism. They will come to understand the meaning of severing old ties between themselves. They will learn Washington's real interests: raw materials, non-Arab oil, markets and a Russia servicing debts in dollars. They will wake up. And Gorbachev may, perhaps, have another chance.

IKEDA: It is characteristically bold of you to foresee Gorbachev's return. Though I consider his actual return to power problematic, in terms of his ideas of a middle position between the dualities of capitalism and socialism, of federation and confederation, I can envision his symbolic return.

When I call his perestroika a revolution, I have more in mind than a mere shift from socialism to capitalism. Of course, it includes the introduction of capitalistic elements; but that is only a part of perestroika. I believe Gorbachev aimed to reform society as a whole, including human awareness itself. The Soviet Union as it was at the time when perestroika was initiated represented the final stage of a social revolution without a human revolution. Lenin's New Economic Policy of the 1920s was an attempt to move in the direction of capitalism through purely economic measures. I am fully aware of the magnitude of even that task. But we must remember that Gorbachev's perestroika started not with economic liberalization, but with reinstatement of the freedom of speech.

Ironically, perestroika itself created the very conditions that now enable people to criticize and attack it. Still, though maligned and battered, perestroika is far from dead.

The newspaper *Nezavisimaya Gazeta* reported on the Gorbachev phenomenon in words to this effect: Russia likes to insult and kill great people. Later, it loves them and sighs and sheds tears of emotion. Gorbachev, our liberator, was fated to be beaten black and blue ... Attacking Gorbachev from all sides is a fearful sign of the psychological sickness of society. People incapable of appreciating the great are incapable of governing the nation well. Society can understand nothing important if it cannot comprehend Gorbachev's thoughts and actions.

You yourself say, 'The peoples of the former Soviet Union will come to see what capitalism means for peripheral areas when they themselves become such peripheral zones of global capitalism.' Experienced Soviet watchers were astounded by the rapid tempo at which the emergence of Gorbachev, the speedy development of perestroika, the attempted putsch, the dissolution of the Communist Party, the collapse of the Union and then the establishment of the Commonwealth of Independent States took place. It was as if a pendulum, out of control, were swinging with full force in one direction. When it goes as far as it can – perhaps when it discovers what capitalism means, as you say – it may well start swinging in the opposite direction.

Whither the Formerly Socialist Nations?

IKEDA: An East German who passionately opposed communist rule for many years remarked that, after reunification, it seemed as if what he had thought to be the long battle for the construction of a new, free nation had really been waged for nothing more than a strong Deutschmark. By toppling communist governments throughout Eastern Europe, the people demonstrated irresistible power. But if their liberated energy creates only greed-driven, casino capitalism, we may be witnessing another of history's cruel jokes.

In his essay 'The End of History?', Francis Fukuyama claims that absolute materialism is the fate of an age without ideals. The very idea of an age without ideals – an age of apathy – is terrifying. This is why devising ways of constructively orienting recently liberated energy in Eastern Europe is one of the most pressing problems now facing us.

GALTUNG: Today the former socialist countries are spiritual vacuums open to the intrusions of all kinds of charlatans, including preachers of the end of history. The belief that history may be ending can only accelerate the emergence of fascism in these countries. If fascism does arise, it may be partly to control the working class and stimulate it to produce for the upper classes and for Western nations (for Japan too, perhaps), and partly to erect new barricades against an affluent, arrogant and expansionist West.

Though obviously the choice is theirs, we are all entitled to our opinions. My own wish is that the former socialist nations will come to consider themselves parts of the Third World, united in solidarity with nations now peripheral to capitalism. Because it is superior

to centralized planning, they should not reject the market system.
They should, however, strive to break out of peripheral status and
attempt a better synthesis of market and planned economy.

In doing this, they can learn much from a report entitled 'The
Challenge of the South' by the South Commission, of which Julius
Nyerere, a leading light in the founding of the Organization of African
Unity, was chairman. One of the basic conclusions of the report
is that nations of the so-called South should cooperate among
themselves instead of waiting in line for favors from the West. Such
waiting is degrading and the opposite of development. The
South–South cooperation recommended for Africa should take the
form of East–East cooperation in Eastern Europe. Though it may
seem attractive at first, being no more than distant provinces of the
opulent European Union looks much less appealing when actually
experienced and when all independence has been abandoned and
all detailed plans originate in Brussels, Bonn and Washington.

IKEDA: You are quite right to criticize the affluent West for arrogance
and expansionist motives. Still another point deserving castigation
is the diminished view the West often takes of the value of humanity
itself. One reason for this diminution is the persisting habit of
interpreting human beings solely in economic terms, even though
we have already moved out of the industrial and into the post-
industrial society.

Nor is today's economic philosophy on the same high level that
it occupied in the days of the economist Adam Smith (1723–90),
who regarded human commercial activities as inseparable from
human virtue. Approaches like his, which incorporate the fate of
epochs and nations, are preferable to the modern view of business
people, who, though perhaps not always limiting their consideration entirely to their own families or employers, certainly operate
on a reduced scale.

Francis Fukuyama says that in a democratic, capitalist society
like that of the United States, ambitious, talented people prefer
entering the world of business to going into politics, the military,
academia or the church. In other words, the more capable people
are, the more likely they are to become economic creatures – on
the diminished scale I have already noted. This seems unsurpris-
ing, given the characteristically Western tendency to undervalue
human nature.

This same underemphasis on humanity is especially apparent in
the way Western nations react to the Third World and former
colonies. Cultural anthropologists point out the earlier self-sufficiency and deep-rooted cultures of regions that were later colonized.
As the always acute Montaigne pointed out, after everything plun-
derable has been plundered, the colonist's sword chops indigenous

cultures to pieces. This is certainly what was done by colonizing Western powers, who traditionally interpreted everything solely in economic terms. Their attitude persists today in the minds of people who allow economic considerations to dominate their ways of thinking.

Such narrow, superficial views invite internal decadence within the Western nations themselves, including of course Japan. My point is vividly illustrated by the number of wealthy Westerners who have lost sight of the meaning of happiness.

To pioneer a new age, we must alter this interpretation of humanity. We must view human beings whole, not solely in terms of economic aspects. Indeed, restoring wholeness to the human being is one of the most urgent problems facing the world today. The ability to imagine humanity's boundless possibilities must inform our approach to the Third World.

Unification

IKEDA: Various forces have worked for economic unification of the Western European nations. But, as the German experience is showing, opinions about the merits of union are far from homogeneous. The events of the next few years will tell whether President Richard von Weizsacker's assessment was correct: 'Unification is part of a historical process that includes all Europe as the various peoples of the European continent seek liberty and a new peaceful order.'

The fate of unification movements – not just European ones – is of the greatest interest to the whole world. Now that the Cold War infrastructure has collapsed, Europe faces the unprecedented experimental task of creating a new order free of belligerence.

On the basis of your extensive work for peace in Europe, how do you evaluate the changes occurring there and what visions have you for the European future?

GALTUNG: The outlook is very threatening. The total integration of Western Europe and the formation, by the end of the twentieth century, of the European Union, complete with common currency, foreign and defense policies and a European army, are frightening. Old habits die hard. From the Vikings through the Teutonic Knights, the Swedish kings, Napoleon and Kaiser Wilhelm II to Adolf Hitler, Western Europe has dreamed of being able to help itself to whatever it wanted in Eastern Europe. And now a totally disintegrated Eastern Europe is up for grabs.

When I addressed the Political Commission of the European Parliament on this issue in March 1990, I feared that Eastern Europe might be colonized economically, culturally and to some extent politically in a process that might be called Latin Americanization. My fears are being realized. Though it has not started yet, military colonization might well be carried out by peacekeeping forces. As long as its role has remained peacekeeping, not peace-enforcing, the legitimacy of the United Nations has increased – even, to some extent, in what was formerly Yugoslavia. Somalia, on the other hand, shows how interventionist force can backfire.

But I greatly fear a Western European army arrogantly imposing peace on Eastern Europe in the old European tradition. I envision it rapidly deploying forces in the 70 former colonies of the African-Caribbean-Pacific system of the European Union should those colonies rebel in one way or another. It must be remembered that nine of the twelve members of the European Union are former colonial powers. Old habits die hard.

An Islamic – Arab or Turkish, or both – union is the obvious response to a Christian-European union. If such a union forms, I can imagine a European army – perhaps nuclear-armed – poised against an Islamic counterpart. Or there might develop a triangular confrontation, with these two plus a Slavic-Orthodox union headed by Russia. All of this has crystallized in the triadic fighting in the former Yugoslavia among Orthodox Catholics, Roman Catholics and Muslims.

In spite of these alarming visions, however, if Eastern Europe and the former Soviet Union are treated as equals by the West and are allowed to take advantage of their own possibilities, a more positive future could result from the formation of a soft confederation in the form of pan-European cooperation extending from the Atlantic coast to Kamchatka. The United Nations Economic Commission for Europe can provide a sound basis for such cooperation. The Helsinki process and the Conference on Security and Cooperation in Europe (CSCE) have created some excellent military and political institutions. The Council of Europe deals with cooperation in cultural affairs and human rights. Both the CSCE and the Council of Europe have parliamentary assemblies. Given such organizations, even the dream of direct pan-European elections might be realizable. In other words, *There Are Alternatives!*; but whether they will be chosen remains to be seen.

To be sure, a pan-European confederation would involve an immense population of 850 million. But I find this a source of little alarm, because the numerous prevailing contradictions and conflicts in the area make united aggressive action abroad unlikely. Whereas the European Union is cohesive enough to pose a danger, a pan-European confederation would not be.

IKEDA: When all is said and done, the formation of small, exclusivist blocs must be avoided. The creation of large, regional, supernational blocs, a development that seems likely in the years to come, may be viewed as a stage in the construction of the next world order. In any event, we must bear in mind the importance of working together with the United Nations (obviously not necessarily in the form in which it exists today).

Our epoch requires an open system in which various regions react with each other on a footing of equality. As I have repeatedly stressed in the past, the unilateral relations of the colonial period offer absolutely no hopeful future prospects for a new world order. They invite only confusion and conflict.

The Twentieth Century

IKEDA: The twentieth century has in a sense been an age of unprecedented tragedy resulting from two global wars, revolutions, counter-revolutions and the cruel totalitarianism of Nazism and Stalinism. As the century draws to a close, we all face the serious problems of evaluating the period that has gone before and determining the course we must follow in the years to come.

GALTUNG: My sense of realism tells me that the twentieth century will go down in history as a period of war, of direct violence and of revolution both in protest against and in defense of structural violence. At present, now that the Cold War has ended, much of the planet enjoys freedom. But another kind of totalitarianism still prevails, the totalitarianism of those who want the entire world to conform to the formula of Western-style democracy and unrestrained market economics.

To some observers, the triumph of democracy and the free market signifies the attainment of a goal and the end of history. The outlook is less rosy, however, in the light of the records of democracies in terms of war. Of course, being at the pinnacle of power and prosperity, they have generally preferred to share rule among themselves in concerts, alliances, communities, even unions, instead of warring against each other. But they have engaged in wars of colonialism, slavery, suppression, punishment and intervention everywhere else. World War I was fought between democracies, of sorts. Far from being peaceful, their record is filled with belligerence.

Nor is the record of capitalism itself any better. Rich capitalist countries are good at exporting their own problems – the so-called negative externalities – and in so doing exerting pernicious influences on their peripheries. Fascism in Southern Europe, communism in Eastern Europe and the two together in Southeastern Europe arose in reaction to expansionist pressure from capitalist, Protestant, Northwestern Europe.

Everyone wants to be their own master; no one wants to be merely the tail-end of a causal chain originating elsewhere. Today Japan is clearly experiencing the totalitarianism of a United States demanding what it calls free trade (in fact it is managed trade) – a stance, incidentally, diametrically opposite to the one the US itself adopted in the second half of the nineteenth century, much to its own advantage.

If we are to seek meaning for the last decade of the twentieth century, it must be in this doctrine: the totalitarianism of democracy-market is another utopian recipe; it must not be considered a suitable replacement for Stalinist and Hitlerist totalitarianism. The democracy-market shoe fits some; but, as we shall soon see, it can pinch too.

From the standpoint of what, with habitual self-congratulation, the ostensibly developed nations call the First World, the twentieth century has been an age of unprecedented tragedy: two world wars and the Holocaust. But for other parts of the world, it has been an age of liberation – no matter how messy – from nineteenth-century and earlier colonialism. The twentieth century looks sometimes tragic, sometimes epic and liberating, sometimes comic and sometimes even farcical, depending on the viewpoint.

In terms of its effects on the female half of humanity, however, the twentieth century has been truly revolutionary. The feminist revolution originated in the United States. It is a gift to humanity; it and environmental awareness are the only true revolutions to come out of that country. The events of 1776 and the following years were only part of the usual western hemisphere story of colonials refusing to share the spoils of repression and exploitation with their mother-lands – in this case, Britain. Furthermore, the ideas behind the American Revolution were predominantly Greek and French.

The feminist revolt, and to a large extent environmental awareness, however, are genuinely American. Interestingly, they have emerged in a country where the working class is so abominably exploited that the products it manufactures are often not good enough for export. Treat the workers like disposable junk and you get junk work. The United States today shows how exploitation brings its own retribution: though it may be tempting in the short run, its ill effects quickly overtake the exploiters. Countries that treat their working classes better, such as Japan, enter the world market with better products.

IKEDA: It is superficial to assert that the collapse of the Soviet Union – hailed in the West as the victory of capitalism and democracy – signifies the end of history. As products of the so-called

Modern Age, both socialism and capitalism have grown from the same root. The French poet Paul Valery (1871–1945) characterized European (modern) civilization as a culture of expansionism demanding the maximum in authority, capital, production efficiency and external alterations of nature. Since both capitalism and socialism are rooted in the soil of this civilization, the downfall of one or the other cannot possibly signify the end of history.

Our task now is to examine the merits and demerits of our history frankly and to correct whatever has gone wrong. The post-Cold War world demands that we revise the orientation of expansionism that has crippling or in some other way deleterious effects. We must take civilization beyond the 'modern' into a new stage.

Respect for human rights must be our guide. All peoples must come to realize and assimilate within themselves the idea of the supreme importance of human life. As the US Scientist Linus Pauling (1901–94) and I wholeheartedly agreed in our dialogue ('A Lifelong Quest for Peace'), the twenty-first century must be devoted to respect for the value of life. All systems and ideologies must be reexamined from the standpoint of human rights and, where necessary, reoriented to accord with respect for those rights. I consider this process the most important task facing us today. We of Soka Gakkai International are devoted to the well-being of the human race and to the human revolution, because of our conviction that success in this undertaking means true historical development.

CHAPTER 3

The Feasibility of Nonviolence

Gandhi: Optimism

IKEDA: In February 1992 I was invited to deliver an address entitled 'Toward a World without War – Gandhi-ism and the Modern World' to the Gandhi Memorial Hall, New Delhi. In discussing things the twenty-first century can learn from the Gandhi heritage, I stressed four elements: optimism, activism, populism and holistic vision. Because it is of pivotal importance to the Gandhian philosophy of nonviolence, a few words must be said about the distinctive traits of Gandhi's brand of optimism. First, it is not relativism determined by objective analyses of circumstances. Instead it is an unconditional, indestructible faith in humanity, a faith born of justice, nonviolence and penetrating self-observation.

Vaclav Havel manifests a radiant optimism similar to the kind typified by Mahatma Gandhi. He has always maintained the faith evident in some remarks in his book *Disturbing the Peace*: 'Hope is not prognostication. It is an orientation of the spirit, an orientation of the heart ... It is not the conviction that something will turn out well, but the certainty that something makes sense, regardless of how it turns out.'

I believe that Mr Havel's optimism can help us understand the distinction between the weakling's nonviolence, engendered by timidity, and the truly noble nonviolence of the strong and courageous.

GALTUNG: I agree entirely with you that optimism was a basic condition for the astonishing major struggles that Gandhi carried out in only one lifetime: the battle for home rule (*swaraj*); his work to elevate the people in general and particularly the self-reliant, small, coherent communities that he called 'oceanic circles' (*sarvodaya*); his battle to improve the condition of the casteless (to whom Gandhi gave the name *harijan*, or children of God); his work to raise the status of women; his efforts in the name of equality on behalf of Indians in South Africa; his not-very-successful strivings for peace between Indian Hindus and Muslims; and most important of all his devoted support for and development of nonviolence (*satyagraha*) as the one valid approach to the attainment of all his other goals.

And he successfully attained most of those goals. India won home rule and became independent. Though perhaps not a success in India, the concept of *sarvodaya* has been an inspiration to peoples all over the world. Within India, the status of the casteless and of women has improved. Early in the twentieth century, Gandhi made great forward strides in South Africa, where he planted the idea of nonviolence as more productive than the violent tactics sometimes employed there. Moreover, now a part of many cultures in many parts of the world, nonviolence has played a significant part in the liberation of Eastern Europe from the double scourge of Stalinism and nuclearism.

The accomplishment of even a fraction of this program would have been impossible without optimism, imagination and deep faith in the potential of the human being. Gandhi had his goal fixed in his mind and knew that the road to peace was nothing other than peace itself.

IKEDA: The Gandhian combination of idealist and man of practical action finds startlingly vivid manifestation in the famous Salt March of 1930, when Gandhi led thousands of people to the seashore to make their own salt in protest against a cruel tax imposed by the British colonial authorities. (The ordinary people are said to have cried out 'Long live the salt thief!' in praise of and gratitude to Gandhi.) In standing up nonviolently against wrong and violent governmental practices Gandhi demonstrated the unfailing unity with the ordinary people that was indispensable to his own original way of thinking.

A comparison between the two shows Gandhi to have been much more practical than the novelist Leo Tolstoy (1928–1910), another advocate of nonviolence whom Gandhi greatly respected. The Russian writer's thoroughgoing, ascetic brand of nonviolence was greatly praised by intellectuals all over the world but failed to find a large following among the ordinary masses, as Gandhi's leadership did.

Though stubbornly faithful to his main principles, Gandhi was pragmatic in all other matters, which he preferred to treat case by case. Albert Einstein referred to Gandhi as the greatest political genius of our times precisely because of his ability to maintain a subtle balance between the ideal and the practical. This ability found concrete embodiment in the nonviolent resistance movement.

Gandhi: Nonviolence versus Structural Violence

IKEDA: Reading your '1989 Fall in East Europe: What Happened and Why?', I was especially fascinated by your explanation of the

bloodlessness – everywhere, except in Romania – of these revolutions. In the past, the struggle for liberty in Europe has usually been
anything but nonviolent. During the disturbances in Hungary in
1956, the Communist authorities considered a single Molotov
cocktail tossed by dissidents justification for military intervention.
A number of factors account for the generally pacific nature of the
events of 1989. One is certainly a sudden and widespread acceptance
of Gandhi's idea of nonviolence. This acceptance was greatly
stimulated by successful peaceful black movements in the United
States and South Africa.

I see two kinds of political power at play in the world today. The
external might of money and arms can be called hard power.
Benign, internally-based people power is soft power. In much of
Eastern Europe, the might of people profoundly sympathetic to
Gandhian ideas resisted military-backed oppression, thus allowing
soft power to triumph bloodlessly.

Gandhian nonviolence has proved itself effectual under one set
of contemporary circumstances. Can it prove equally effective in
combating what you call structural violence in the Third World?
As you point out in your celebrated thesis 'A Structural Theory of
Imperialism', imperial control inevitably generates violence. Can
nonviolence work in an imperial structure dominated by
center–periphery relations in which the center is strong and the
periphery weak?

GALTUNG: Gandhi answered direct violence with nonviolent defense;
he answered structural violence with nonviolent revolution. You
ask whether these methods can work in an imperial structure. It
certainly worked in the Soviet Tsarist-Bolshevik structure, one of
the most brutal of all the world's empires. Unfortunately, however,
parts of the former British empire that liberated themselves from
British rule have forgotten how they won their victory and have fallen
to squabbling violently among themselves, particularly Muslims
against Hindus.

The basic formula for the effectiveness of these techniques is
twofold: to strengthen the periphery (that is, the weak) and to weaken
the center (the strong). By the end of their era, the elites of the post-
Stalinist imperial structure were demoralized enough to be far
more amenable to popular influence than Western elites assumed.
Ignoring the severe criticism heaped on visitors to socialist countries
during the Cold War, I often met post-Stalinist elites, pointed out
to them the absurdity and ineffectualness of their system and
suggested alternatives to it: democratic and more green, social
democrat and 'Japanist'. In my experience, nothing is as successfully subversive as suggesting a feasible alternative. After 1980,
post-Stalinist regimes were seriously weakened from within by

protest and mass movements, like Polish Solidarity, and were presented with clear alternatives, such as human rights, free elections and a market economy. Although it may take some time to do so, violence always rebounds on the violent.

Stronger than ever before, however, Western imperialism is increasingly burdening the Third World with debts and dependencies. I can understand why Panamanians, Iraqis, Serbians and so on resist the idea of obedient service to Western elites and want to find their own ways to a better, more just world. Nonetheless, fighting violence with violence is both ethically wrong and politically foolish.

This is attempting to play into the hands of the system, which knows very well how to administer violence. With centuries of experience in punishing peoples to keep them in line, the strong centers repay a hundredfold all violence inflicted on them. Approaching them with nonviolence, on the other hand, is tantamount to addressing their best attributes. Gandhi did this to the British. And he succeeded with many, though not with the most hardened Churchillian elites. Had they been nonviolent, General Noriega of Panama, Saddam Hussein of Iraq, and Slobodan Milosevic of Serbia might by now have attained the dignity and justice they sought for their people. They would have had to redefine their goals in keeping with the doctrines of a more nonviolent society. As things are, by intervening violently these men destroyed themselves directly and indirectly.

Strengthening the weak necessitates a detailed basic vision, not imposed from above but evolved through thousands of dialogues. The strong center penetrates the mind of the weak periphery. The periphery must counter this nonviolently by evolving its own consciousness. In many parts of the world today, women are doing this in their struggle against patriarchy, one of the most vicious forms of structural violence. And soon children all over the world may start doing it against rule by adults.

Then – though this might just as well be the first step – peripheral elements must meet, compare experiences and work for integration by combating fragmentation, segmentation and marginalization of the system. Though much work remains, Third World countries have done this. The Non-Govermental Organizations (NGO) Forum at the human rights conference in Vienna in June 1993 is a fine case in point. Peripheral countries must trade more among themselves, as Nordic countries once did. Unlike vertical, exploitative relations, horizontal trading partnerships create wealth for all levels of society.

At the same time, equally – or even more – important, the citizens of countries on the periphery must liberate themselves from their own, often very oppressive elites. All these processes are going on in the world today. The end is not yet in sight, but I am optimistic.

IKEDA: You take a stern view of the baleful effects the West has had on much of the modern world. Whereas I understand what you mean, I evaluate modern Western values of liberty, democracy and human rights somewhat differently.

Of course, those values evolved parallel with abominable colonial exploitation. Energetic objections to the fifth centennial celebrations of Columbus's arrival in the Americas proved that indigenous peoples remain painfully aware of the sufferings Europeans inflicted on them.

Reality often fails to reflect proclaimed lofty ideals, and human beings tend to be inconsistent. The French philosopher and celebrated Christian humanist Ernest Renan (1823–92) was sympathetic to Nazi racial theories. Albert Schweitzer (1875–1965), the so-called Sage of the Forest, was oddly ambivalent on the topic of racial discrimination.

Realizing human fallibility, I prefer to cling to a few minimal values as being of universal worth and efficacy. Fundamental among those values are liberty, democracy and a justly-articulated expression of inviolable human rights.

You regard such abstractions as double-edged swords that, depending on the uses to which they are put, can accelerate structural violence. I agree with you to the extent of insisting that the realization of these ideal values be carried out with the utmost prudence. Liberty, democracy and human rights are common human properties that, formulated with latitude to encompass the maximum diversity of needs, will some day be made available to all.

For all its faults, Western thought has articulated and stimulated awareness of such fundamental rights. The best people in the West strive to realize something like the Gandhian ideal and, when they fail, attempt to rectify their own shortcomings. As Arthur M. Schlesinger Jr. says in *The Disunity of America*:

> There remains, however, a crucial difference between the Western tradition and the others. The crimes of the West have produced their own antidotes. They have provoked great movements to end slavery, to raise the status of women, to abolish torture, to combat racism, to defend freedom of inquiry and expression, to advance personal liberty and human rights.

Of course, occurrences like the riots in Los Angeles in 1992 cast doubt on the efficacy of the 'means' of correction. Nonetheless, as I said, I believe the best Westerners – among whom we may include Mr Schlesinger – work hard to make the Gandhian approach even more effective.

GALTUNG: I agree with your assessment. The name 'Europe' comes from the Assyrian word *erp*, which means darkness. Europe and the US – that is, the West – have two different sides, like the Roman god Janus who had two faces and two voices. In addition to its soft, compassionate aspect, which I thoroughly appreciate, Europe has a hard, violent side. Helping the West liberate itself from its darker aspects is the problem. I am afraid that the soft will serve as an alibi for the dark.

IKEDA: The solution to the problem is to search out the ultimate causes of those dark aspects. Manichaeanism, a syncretic sect of Persian Zoroastrianism, attempted to win the minds of its followers by dividing the phenomenal world into a clear dualism of good and evil. It was not, of course, alone in this. Certain kinds of people have always been attracted by the spellbinding lucidity of dualisms such as good and evil, light and dark, friend and foe, love and hate and so on. Such people tend to seek easy answers and to find intolerable the psychological operations inherent in dialogue (in the Socratic sense) and speculation for the sake of plumbing the truth of things. Observable in all places at all times, this weakness makes the human beings who demonstrate it ripe prey for the persuasive techniques of groups like the unprincipled ancient Athenian demagogues.

I find the tendency to seek easy answers without penetrating examination more dominant in the monotheistic than in the polytheistic religions. I am aware of the history of opposition and disagreement between Manichaeanism and Roman Catholicism and realize that the two probably should not be discussed as if they were of the same order. But, as was the case between new and old beliefs within Christianity itself, the opposition between Manichaeanism and Roman Catholicism bred especially virulent animosity precisely because the two sides involved in it were very closely related. This seems to me to be fundamental to monotheistic traditions. Probably the tradition of thinking in terms of dualities and of making facile discriminatory distinctions contributes to the hard, cruel aspects you find in the behavior of Europe. Horrifying discrimination such as so-called racial purification in the former Yugoslavia and the emergence of historically retrogressive ultra-rightists and racists in Germany, France and Italy indicate the extent to which this dark tradition persists.

To liberate modern humanity – and not just Europeans – from the spell of such attitudes, we must look for the evil at fault within human beings. We must make ourselves realize thoroughly that the evil inside is primary and the evil outside only secondary in significance. The most important thing to learn from the experiences of the twentieth century is this: whether the issue is racial, as in the case of fascism, or class-related, as in the case of communism, attempting to trace primary causes of evil to external factors invites tragedy and slaughter. Transcending inner evil is both our most urgent duty for the twenty-first century and the essential goal of all reform movements. This is what we of Soka Gakkai International refer to as the 'human revolution'.

Gandhi: An Unclouded Eye

IKEDA: Gandhi was one of the first to predict accurately the downfall of political structures based on power and violence – like those of the former Soviet Union and its satellite nations in East Europe. In December 1931, on the shores of Lake Leman in Switzerland, he paid a sick call on the French writer Romain Rolland (1866–1944), who, like many people of the period, was spellbound by socialism as the star of hope in the darkness of an apparently collapsing capitalist system. To Rolland, Gandhi said:

> What is happening in Russia is an enigma. I have not discussed Russia very much, but I have a deep mistrust of the ultimate success of the experiment being carried out there. It seems to me that it is a challenge to nonviolence. It appears to be succeeding, but behind its success lies force, violence ... When Indians are exposed to Russian influence, it leads them into extreme intolerance.

Without the flood of information we have today, Gandhi relied on his own experience and his unclouded eye to penetrate to the evil behind the violence and intolerance of Bolshevism.

Faith in the infinite possibilities of the inner human being was the source of his perspicacity. He represented the diametric opposite of Marxism-Leninism, with its exclusively exterior approach to humanity and its dictum that human beings are no more than the sum of their social conditions. Mahatma Gandhi's approach provides fundamental answers to questions about revolutionizing individual human beings and society.

GALTUNG: The comments Gandhi made during his visit to Romain Rolland impress me, too, with their great foresight. For Gandhi, ends and means always had to be consistent and subject to the same ethical principles: violence can only breed violence. Similarly, as can be seen in good relations between the British and the Indians today, nonviolence breeds nonviolence. Certainly national Bolshevism bred only violence for the Russians and the inhabitants of the whole Soviet empire. Where life is not held sacred, death is the harvest.

But the strictures Gandhi laid at Russia's doors are applicable in the West, too. The French Revolution, which is usually celebrated as a great liberation, was actually excessively cruel and bloody. The connections between the Revolution and Napoleon's wars for the sake of European domination are generally overlooked. The United States was born in blood. Genocide was conducted against maybe 10 million indigenous Americans in the period 1500–1900, who were later confined to reservations, a very vicious form of structural violence. Many Native Americans remain on reservations today, with no hope of an end to their misery in sight. The struggle for independence between 1776 and 1812 was mostly violent, as was the cruel and bloody Civil War of 1861–5, the main goal of which was preservation of the Union; abolition of slavery was only a secondary issue.

The goals of these revolutionary struggles could have been attained nonviolently, without encouraging and strengthening the strains of violence inherent in the people waging them. These strains were, however, reinforced and manifested themselves later as colonialism, slavery and military interventions, of which the United States has been guilty more than 200 times. The French have intervened militarily at least 14 times in the affairs of their former colonies. As this suggests, what Gandhi said about violence in Russia is applicable to other countries as well.

IKEDA: Your strictures on Western nations are justified. I think it is important, however, to point up a characteristic of Marxist-socialist society that greatly reduces the likelihood of its being successful, given the unreformed nature of much of humanity. Gandhi himself said:

> This socialism is as pure as crystal. It, therefore, requires crystal-like means to achieve it. Impure means result in an impure end … Therefore only truthful, nonviolent and pure-hearted socialists will be able to establish a socialistic society in India and the world. (Gandhi, *All Men Are Brothers*, p. 76)

Since this is true, there can be no doubt of the fundamental necessity of the human revolution. Marxist socialism interprets the human being as an aggregate of social relations. Having combined human concerns and social interests – thus eliminating the former – Marxist socialism concentrates solely on reforming the means of production, which are regarded as the foundation of all social relations.

Gandhi saw that the socialist formula, in which first priority went to the reformation of the political-economic system, was an inversion. He realized that human beings are the true starting point and that, to be long-lasting, all external revolutions must arise from internal revolutions. The more violent the times, the more unflinchingly human beings must direct their searching gazes inward. This is the eternal theme to which he would have us all return.

GALTUNG: I agree entirely. What you say has a great message for left-wing people who, in their hatred of capitalism and the military establishment, either forget or never develop compassion for the victims of revolutions. The full human capability for both outer dialogue with others and inner dialogue with the self provides a good starting point for searching inward gazes. In my view, together the inner and outer dialogues constitute the essence of the praxis of Buddhism. In the Soviet experience, both were neglected. Instead of an inner dialogue examining assumptions, there was only dogmatic social determinism; instead of an outer dialogue, there was often violent action. What the Soviets had was no more than a parody, a caricature, of the kind of revolution Gandhi initiated. Of course, the Soviet system failed. History is a sometimes harsh, but just judge.

Gandhi: Religious Breadth

IKEDA: I think it was only once that Mahatma Gandhi said that he himself might conceivably be called a Buddhist. I understand that you regard Gandhi as the legitimate Indian heir to Shakyamuni's philosophy and see Buddhism reflected in his opposition to the caste system. Precisely in what aspects of Gandhi's thoughts and deeds do you trace Buddhist influences? What are your thoughts on his religious views and his attitude toward faith? When, as sometimes occurred, he was criticized for being eclectic, he is said to have replied, 'It [my faith] is a faith based on the broadest possible toleration' (*Young India*, 22 December 1927). The attitude expressed in this statement suggests that Gandhi was far from sectarian.

GALTUNG: Gandhi was very ecumenical. He was a *banya*, a member of the *vaishya* (commercial) Hindu caste. In some basic respects, Buddhism is a reform movement within the great Hindu tradition and therefore shares many common traits with Hinduism. The word 'Hinduism' itself is a most inadequate term for a vast conglomerate of profound philosophies. I see Gandhi's Buddhist inclinations in three directions within this conglomerate.

First, of course, in his insistence on nonviolence (*ahimsa*), not as a mere ideal but as a practice applied to all forms of life – among animals, too; not just cows, though the sacredness of cows is symbolically important. I agree in principle with and wish I myself could emulate Gandhi's vegetarianism, which is in keeping with the doctrine of *ahimsa*.

His second Buddhist-like orientation is to be found in his rejection of the vertical caste system, though he retained the *varna* – occupation, or *Beruf* to give it its German name – as hereditary. Gandhi felt that being born into an occupation is like being born into a gender: it is useful; it eliminates the need to make a choice and enables the individual to concentrate on spiritual development.

He was very strongly opposed, however, to the verticality of the caste order, according to which the casteless and the lowest caste (*shudras*) were treated atrociously. He envisioned a horizontal caste system in which all occupations are treated equally in a symbiotic union of diverse elements. Each profession should have dignity; and, to the maximum extent possible, the dignity of all should be equal.

Third, he was fascinated by small communities, autonomous villages that resemble the Buddhist idea of the *sangha*, or community of believers. Gandhi's community includes the temple and the tank or well. It provides enough for everybody's needs, but not for everybody's greed. There is neither misery at the bottom nor excessive accumulation of wealth at the top. His ideas were a far cry from those represented by big cities run by *brahmins*, *kshatriyas* and *vaishyas* and entirely compatible with Hinduism.

These three – and other – departures from mainstream Hinduism cost Gandhi his life. His assassin, Nathuram Godse, is sometimes described as a fanatic, sometimes as an orthodox Hindu. Apparently he was neither. He was simply a man who considered Gandhi a traitor to both Hinduism and to the nascent modern (meaning more Western) India. Himself a *brahmin* from the Hindu stronghold of Pune near Bombay, Godse believed that post-colonial India needed the vertical caste system and a strong military in the old *kshatriya* (warrior) tradition. His opinions, which coincided with those of all Indian governments except Morarji Desai's short-lived Janata regime of the 1970s, contrasted sharply with Gandhi's. The result of this contrast was Gandhi's death.

Gandhi drew inspiration from Judaism, Christianity and Islam. He wanted to learn from them and pointed out their similarities in order to help them coalesce so that higher goals could be achieved. While looking Westward to these religions, he seems to have turned his back on such great Far Eastern faiths as Daoism, Confucianism and Shintoism and, by and large, was silent on Buddhism.

IKEDA: The three departures you outline indicate Gandhi's practicality and sense of order. Perhaps Buddhism and Hinduism refined his rare personal traits. No doubt he was thoroughly knowledgeable about the formation and management of human society and the nature of the conditions enabling human beings to discover opportunities for fulfillment and the manifestation of their abilities.

From the viewpoint of European liberty and equality, his condoning the idea of a hereditary calling associated with the caste system while rejecting the system itself may seem inconsistent. But he may have wished to emphasize the stabilizing effect of the hereditary calling and the likeliness of disorder in an excessively fluid society.

In principle, freeing people from the fetters of the past is an excellent idea. In actuality, however, human needs and desires cannot be satisfied by means of liberty and equality alone. In spite of freedom, the human mind inevitably becomes dissatisfied and insecure. The Industrial Revolution in Europe freed people from the older agrarian system but inspired insecurity that played a large part in stimulating population displacements and urbanization. Of course, a stagnant society is no better than a society in constant flux. Gandhi's preference for a small community may have arisen partly from his understanding of the modern urban malaise, with its generation gaps and high crime rates, both outcomes of too much violent change and the inability of some parts of the population to keep up with the rest.

Gandhi was a gradualist, not a radical. He thought good changes take time – they move at a snail's pace. This too is part of his sense of practicality and order, in which I see a reflection of the Buddhist idea of the middle way.

Buddhist wisdom has clearly and accurately perceived the middle way between existence and nonexistence; between pain and pleasure; and between the doctrine of eternity, according to which conditioned elements themselves are eternal, and the doctrine of annihilation. His practical approach leads me to believe that Gandhi, too, perceived this middle way.

GALTUNG: I am not quite sure; not always. Since big cities and big industry were instruments of British imperialism, Gandhi's negative views of them are understandable. Is it not possible, however, to humanize cities and industry? Cities can become confederations of relatively autonomous neighborhoods. Industries can reform in a similar fashion: technologies that degrade neither human users nor the natural environment can be evolved. Large factories and office buildings may give way to more work at home. Gandhi proposed nonviolence as an alternative to the choice between violence and capitulation. Cities and industries remodeled as I suggest would provide similar alternatives to the choice between cities and villages and to the choice between industry and cottage industry and agriculture. As you say, Gandhi perceived the middle way, but he did not develop it with regard to villages versus cities.

It is to be traced more in his spirit than in his words and deeds. The millions of people whom he inspired must work out the middle way for themselves. Work toward that end is being done all over the world, especially under the inspiration of the Green movement.

The Death Penalty

IKEDA: The question of the death penalty is a vexed one. As a Buddhist, I oppose capital punishment as an extreme form of state-inflicted violence. Nothing justifies deliberately depriving another human being of life. Justice does sometimes miscarry; when it does, the innocent may be wrongly executed. The crime-deterrence of the death penalty is widely claimed but remains unproven. Statistics fail to show unusually high rates of vicious crime in societies without the death penalty.

Many of the world's great thinkers and artists have argued passionately against capital punishment. The turbulent nature of his own times in no way inhibited the French novelist Victor Hugo (1802–85) from advocating its abolition. He put into the mouth of one of his literary creations his own castigations of judges who officiously, coolly and complacently order executions, thus condemning the criminal to death and his surviving family to poverty and misery. Hugo insisted that life imprisonment is sufficient punishment for any crime.

On the other side of the issue, Goethe, who seems to have considered vengeance and capital punishment as kinds of self-defense, thought revenge, if legalized, would replace capital punishment. Mahatma Gandhi, who was far above revenge, said it is braver to forgive than to punish an enemy. His attitude is essential to all considerations of violence, including the death penalty.

GALTUNG: No society worthy of being called civilized would indulge in the barbarism of the death penalty. Perhaps we might profitably approach this important topic within the general context of the theory of crime and punishment. The crucial issue is whether we deal with the issue horizontally or vertically. In the former instance, the wrongdoer is directly confronted in order to find out what went wrong and how karma may be improved for the sake of the future. To compensate for the crime, the guilty party must repay stolen money, heal wounds and so on. Actually a great deal more of the world's wrongs are settled in this way than appears to be the case on the surface. The horizontal approach is the mature way of combining reconciliation with self-improvement. Such is not, however, the way of the legal systems in force today.

Not everyone is capable of coping with the horizontal approach. Asking a raped woman or the bereaved survivors of a murder victim to forgive an evildoer is expecting very, very much. Such people may well desire revenge. Indeed, the purpose of imprisonment is to keep the vengeful out as well as to punish the evildoer by keeping him or her in, thus preventing further crime. The vertical approach to dealing with crime culminates in the death penalty, which gives the state godlike attributes as the granter or taker of life itself.

Like you, I oppose the death penalty because I believe no one has the right to destroy life. In addition, I am against it because it legitimizes killing. As you suggest, far from preventing crime, the death penalty seems to foster it. Moreover, a state that considers itself justified in taking life at home will have even less hesitation in taking it abroad. The hundreds of military interventions the United States has perpetrated are a good illustration of my meaning.

Sublimating Aggressive Instincts

IKEDA: Cultivating the united, pacific world opinion essential to lasting peace depends on education. By education, I mean more than schooling. Opportunities for education are limitless and present themselves in all aspects of life.

Major topics that must form part of peace education everywhere include recognition of the universality of human rights. A good way to cultivate awareness of this universality is to illustrate the many similarities linking human cultures in all parts of the world. This can be done by calling attention to certain apparent universal attitudes. For instance, the comment in the Confucian *Analects*, 'Do not do unto others what you would not have them do unto you' is reflected practically verbatim in a remark made many centuries after Confucius by Voltaire (1694–1778) in his defense of the judicial martyr Jean Calas.

Every opportunity must be seized to educate people about the horrors of war and the blessings of peace. The Hiroshima Peace Memorial exhibition of photographs depicting the aftermath of the atomic bombings is an unforgettable antiwar educational experience. We believe that the widely discussed exhibit of pictures entitled 'The Iron Tempest' that our organization has compiled from works inspired by memories of survivors of the Battle of Okinawa of 1945 serves the same purpose.

The ultimate goal of antiwar education must be the purification – through mental and physical experiences – of the human drives that generate bellicosity. The American philosopher William James once said human instincts for domination and conflict – the causes of war – cannot be eliminated. Even if James was right, we must at least try to sublimate them to higher planes so as to replace war with morality.

GALTUNG: I am afraid I cannot agree entirely with William James. It is interesting to note that thinkers from very belligerent cultures tend to think in terms of human instincts for domination and conflict. The Austrian zoologist Konrad Lorenz (1903–89) and his theory of space and aggressive instincts are a case in point. Since most of them are male, these thinkers would do well to begin their study with the reflection that at least 95 to 98 per cent of all direct violence is committed by men. In other words, perhaps it is male, and not human, inclinations that cannot be overcome.

Some nations and some epochs are much more belligerent and domineering than others. If, like the drives for food and sex, belligerence were instinctive, we should expect it to be more uniformly distributed in time and space. With some minor variations, human beings everywhere and in all times eat and drink and engage in sexual activity. The same universality does not apply to war and violence.

Much greater insight is provided by relating the phenomenon of violence to cultures and structures. Some cultures are very dangerous because they consider themselves select or chosen above all others. Such cultures may have become so traumatized that they believe themselves entitled to revenge. Or they may wish to revive past myths or glories. Some structures are either highly repressive or exploitative – or both. Structures of this kind readily elicit revolutionary violence from below or counter-revolutionary violence from above. The combination of so-called chosen cultures and repressive social structures almost invariably and fairly speedily results in direct violence; from below in order to liberate, and from above in order to prevent liberation.

Adherents of 'chosen' cultures and repressive-exploitative structures are certain to call on other explanations of violence – instincts, inherent evil, original sin and so on. Therefore peace education has two primary aspects. One is insight into the roots of violence, wherever they lie. The other and more important aspect, however, is devising ways to overcome, reduce and prevent direct violence. That is what peace studies are all about.

Both aspects of peace education are essential. Studying only violence may make us highly realistic, and highly cynical as well. Studying only peace may make us idealistic but powerless because we become too naive. Instead of siding with the sublimation theory of both William James and Freud, I believe more in the difficult task of re-forming cultures and structures.

Obviously, in connection with peace education, countless concrete measures may be adopted. But underlying them all is the problem you state: 'How do we cultivate respect for the value of peace?' In *The Moral Equivalent of War*, William James offers a positive suggestion: by finding other ways of being heroic. Although it was unknown to James, Gandhi's *satyagraha* is another positive suggestion; precisely a 'moral equivalent of war'.

I certainly see heroism in United Nations peacekeeping forces' exposing themselves to sniper fire while trying to take food to starving civilian populations. True heroism is not killing; it is risking one's own life to prevent killing and to save and enhance life itself. Education should concentrate more on such acts than on military bravery.

Another important area for peace education is making the positive aspects of all religions as widely known as possible. In this, too, Gandhi sets the example. Art, literature and science should be mobilized openly and profoundly for peace (not for propaganda). There is much to do. Much can be done. Ours is to undertake the task.

IKEDA: Yes, the responsibility is ours. And we of Soka Gakkai International approach the educational task on a very fundamental level: the reformation of the inner life. Buddhism analyzes life into ten states: hell, or the world of suffering; hunger, or the state of frustrated desires; animality, or the state in which reason is lost; anger, the state in which life is devoted to conflict and the domination of others; the tranquil humanity state; heaven, or the state in which desires are fulfilled; the state of learning and devotion to self-improvement; the state of realization, or of emotional discovery and satisfaction with one's own world; the altruistic Bodhisattva state[*]; and the Buddha state of enlightenment to the meaning of life and the universe. All of these states are inherent in all life-forms. Contact with a causal factor can cause any one of them to become manifest at any moment.

The first three states are called the Three Evil Paths. Together with the fourth state – anger – they are called the Four Evil Paths. All human impulses to violence and aggressive instincts arise from these four states. Consequently, it behooves each person to learn to control these states and orient them in a correct direction.

---

[*] Bodhisattva state: The ninth of the Ten Worlds, a state characterized by compassion in which one seeks enlightenment both for oneself and for others. In this state one finds satisfaction in devoting oneself to saving others, even at the cost of one's own life. (Adapted from *A Dictionary of Buddhist Terms and Concepts*.)

Of course, cultural quality greatly influences the way in which life in these four evil states manifests itself in society as a whole. For example, accepted conceptions about masculinity lead society and families to educate males to be positive and strong. This often means that the anger state of life is more conspicuous in men than in women.

In extreme terms, war can be described as the condition in which the nation state manipulates society and information so as to evoke and direct the anger aspect of life. Under such circumstances, in the glorified name of state interests, the populace approves of violence and condemns as effeminate all attempts to restrain anger.

Since all the states are inherent in life itself, it is useless to attempt to eliminate the bad ones and leave only the good ones. We must not, however, allow the evil states to run unrestrained. Instead we must attempt to subjugate them to the Law. There are many ways in which this can be done. In sports, for example, a catharsis is effected by subjecting the combative spirit to the rules of the game. Our goal must be to devise as many kinds of sublimation as possible for individuals and for society as a whole.

Gandhi's inner rules converted his anger against injustice and wickedness into his original doctrine of nonviolent disobedience. His 'truth', as he called these rules, was undoubtedly religiously formed. And though he was a Hindu, his practical activities reveal the spirit taught by Shakyamuni.

All Soka Gakkai International activities are based on the idea of the human revolution. Their goal is to reform individual lives through Buddhism and to train human nature by means of culture and education. In the terminology of the Ten States of Life, this goal is to make the Bodhisattva and Buddha states the foundation of life and to subjugate all the other states to them.

As a peace movement on the popular level, Soka Gakkai International and its activities may be considered a contemporary development of Gandhi-ism. Our aim is to create a citadel of peace in the mind of each individual and in this way to educate the masses to love peace and reject violence. This of course demands that each of us realize the impossibility of building true happiness on the unhappiness of others.

CHAPTER 4

Religion as Transformation

Universal Life-resonance

GALTUNG: Buddhism rejects the existence of the soul as an entity. At the same time, it recognizes transmigration. I am interested in the relation between the two.

IKEDA: Buddhism rejects the idea of a persisting self or soul that continues to exist after death. In Japanese this doctrine is called *muga*, or 'nonexistence of self'. Buddhism does, however, teach that the greater force of universal life extends unbroken from the past to the present and into the future, following a regulated cyclical pattern of individual lives and deaths. As your comment implies, Buddhism has successfully merged the two ideas.

GALTUNG: How are we to understand the concept of rebirth without a persisting entity? My own image is that of a flow of energy in which single individual existences – male or female – merge with a diversity of other existences. Our responsibility in connection with the universal force of life is to use the flow of positive good energy to strengthen the inherent Buddha nature. This image evokes another of a boundary-free world in which connections bind together all human beings, humanity and other life-forms, genders, generations, races and classes, nations and countries.

IKEDA: Buddhist philosophy teaches that karma is the element that transmigrates. Karma resulting from deeds, words and thoughts committed by the whole psychosomatic being is deeply ingrained within universal life and transcends individual life and death. According to the doctrine of what are called the Nine Consciousnesses, the karmic aggregate is the Eighth Consciousness (the *alaya vijnana* in Sanskrit; *arayashiki* in Japanese). Extending from the superficial to the deepest levels of life, the Nine Consciousnesses include six levels controlled by the six senses as well as three other deeper levels. Because it represents the karmic aggregate, the Eighth Consciousness is referred to as the Karma Storehouse.

I believe that people today find this doctrine easier to understand if karma is interpreted as latent life-energy with an influence that transcends the individual life in terms of both time and space. Within the depths of life, individual Eighth Consciousnesses can merge to effect exchanges of latent energy.

GALTUNG: I gather you mean that, not limited to a single individual, this energy flows through the lives of all human beings.

IKEDA: That is correct. At its deep levels, the latent energy of life extends to families, ethnic groups and all humanity; thence still further to merge with other forms of life, including nonhuman forms. At the level visible to human eyes, boundaries exist between these forms. Deep down, however, life is integrated and boundary-less.

Karma may be good, bad or neutral. A life manifesting predominantly bad karma is at fate's mercy. The influence of its energy brings misfortune to others and can lead to environmental destruction and even to the annihilation of the human race. It is of the utmost importance to transform bad karma into good karma at the individual level. The transformation of the karma of one individual evokes a similar transformation in other individuals. This process can expand to make possible similar transformations in entire societies, in all humankind and even in the natural environment. This is the meaning of the Soka Gakkai human revolution movement.

Transforming bad karma into good karma cannot be done on the level of the Eighth Consciousness alone. Universal life, which subsumes the Eighth Consciousness, is the Ninth Consciousness (the *amala vijnana*), or the Buddha nature, which, as you say, must be strengthened as much as possible. Once attained, the Buddha state of life purifies and reforms the Eighth Consciousness (Karma Storehouse) and orients all karma toward ultimate good. This is the quintessential meaning of Buddhism.

The individual who perseveres along the path of the human revolution attains a realm of eternally indestructible happiness beyond the life–death cycle. Such a person guides others' innate energy in promising directions and helps them bring forth deeper compassion and wisdom. A tide culminating in the reformation of humanity and our planet is the ultimate goal of the human revolution.

GALTUNG: Your explanation is clearer than any I have ever heard before. But there are two points I should like to clarify still further. Inevitably we manifest both positive and negative energy. How should we deal with negative energy?

IKEDA: On all dimensions, losing to negative force spells unhappiness; it brings loss of life-power, destruction, decline and schism. It results in illness, economic hardships and struggle. War is a concentration of all these sufferings.

Life in the four states that Buddhist philosophy calls the Four Evil Paths is dominated by less-than-human tendencies. These states represent negative energy. In contrast to them, the Four Noble Worlds – Buddhahood, Bodhisattvahood, realization and learning – are conditions in which life generates positive energy. These states spell happiness and fulfillment for human beings and produce the three values advocated by Soka Gakkai philosophy: beauty, gain and goodness.

In a sense, human life and, in particular, work for peace represent struggles between positive and negative energy. Some minus aspects are violence, destruction, schism and hostility; among the positive aspects are nonviolence, creativity, union and harmony. As you have pointed out, throughout human history the triumph of the positive has required each individual to conquer his or her own negative aspects and convert them to positive aspects. Though it might seem circuitous, this is actually the shortest, most direct way to the goal, the attainment of which is the reason for the existence of Buddhism and the human revolution.

GALTUNG: To facilitate the interconnections and mingling of good life-energy we must remove as many barriers and boundaries as possible. Of course, boundaries make for long cuts not shortcuts. Good life-resonance is possible only when the boundary lines between national states and other organizations have been shortened and when unity and solidarity have been achieved. As an example, I might cite your own successful exchanges of ideas and positive energy with Mikhail S. Gorbachev. Boundaries had to be eliminated and space crossed before those exchanges could take place. For one thing, either you had to be free to go to Moscow, or he had to be free to come to Tokyo. I believe that Buddhism agrees with the need to eliminate boundaries.

IKEDA: Yes indeed. This is why I travel widely, trying to bring different parts of the world together.

A major Buddhist tenet teaches what are called the Three Realms of Existence (the realm of the five components, the realm of living beings and the realm of the environment). Each realm embodies boundaries of difference: personal differences, national differences and environmental differences. People all over the world differ radically in terms of their antecedents, endowments, cultures and traditions. Nonetheless, encounters occur in which it is possible to experience profound sympathetic resonances that cross all these boundaries of difference. Comrades and friends advancing toward a common goal draw together naturally and are soon walking side by side.

GALTUNG: You speak of life-resonance. In physics there is such a thing as the phenomenon of resonance. If two tuning forks of the same pitch are placed side by side and one of them is struck, the other will naturally vibrate in resonance.

IKEDA: The same kind of resonance can easily occur between two people whose rhythms are similar. For example, two people who live according to the universal Bodhisattva rhythm overcome boundaries and differences to resonate together. The Buddhist faith may be described as a discipline for putting oneself in agreement – establishing life-resonance – with the universal Buddha nature.

It is generally accepted that, just as scoundrels flock together, so outstanding people associate with other outstanding people. Though starting points differ, a common goal and great faith enable those who work for the lofty aim of world peace to communicate among themselves. This has helped me make many friends all over the world.

A person with powerful life-energy exerts a great influence for orienting companions in a common direction. People of strong faith initiate flows of energy as surely as pressure differential causes air currents to flow from areas of high to areas of low atmospheric pressure. To facilitate encounters making these things possible, we must abbreviate social boundary lines and lower social barriers.

The Interconnectedness of All Things

IKEDA: You have commented that Buddhism is most faithful to the word 'religion' in the sense of the Latin verb from which it derives; that is, *religare*, to bind fast. Certainly the teaching that all natural and social phenomena in the universe are intimately bound together by interdependent causal origination is pivotal to Buddhist thought. You prize this teaching for the power it can provide in promoting world peace and environmental protection. How do Christianity and Islam compare with Buddhism in this connection?

GALTUNG: In my experience, religions come in what may be called hard and soft versions. This applies especially to the three Abrahamitic or semitic religions: Judaism, Christianity and Islam. The hard versions are often related to the idea of a transcendent god, sometimes a male dwelling outside the planet. The softer versions relate to an immanent concept of the sacred within human beings, or, as Buddhists say, inherent in all life. The Latin verb *religare* in this religious context therefore has two distinct connotations. On the one hand, seeking union in a vertical relation with a transcendent god 'up there' always means submissiveness of one kind or another. The softer religions, on the other hand, promote horizontal connections with other beings and ultimately with all life, even in the past and the future.

Because they have a strong transcendent bias, submissiveness and authoritarian patterns come naturally to Judaism, Christianity and Islam. I must hasten to add that this does not apply to Baruch Spinoza, St Francis of Assisi in the Christian church or the great, mystical Sufi tradition in Islam. There is soft in the hard, and hard in the soft.

Though to a lesser degree in the Five Pillars of Islam, in Christianity the Ten Commandments pose a problem. There is no difficulty about some of the commandments: notably those against killing, lying and stealing. But I have problems accepting the strong focus on parental and godly authority and on private property and not coveting it. Of course, covetousness is bad. But, though not condemned in the commandments as stealing, taking something that is not freely given – as is forbidden by Buddhist teachings – may be worse. An example is exploitation: where something is taken, not freely given but not stolen. By tradition or even law, in many places landowners get 70 per cent of the harvest produced by their tenants. Islam at least tries to modify the situation by means of the *zakat*, the third of the Five Pillars of the faith, which was originally a tax but is now a voluntary charitable contribution made by Muslims to the state or community. The decalogue fails to take this kind of thing into consideration.

IKEDA: Because compassionate caring for life in all its forms constitutes a basic part of its philosophy, Buddhism places the admonition against taking life first, in the place of maximum importance, in its list of precepts. In contrast, the Judaeo-Christian decalogue puts 'Thou shalt not kill' in sixth place after five commandments related to submission and obedience to God. Whereas Buddhism respects life in all its forms, Christianity makes a sharp distinction between human and nonhuman life, sometimes respecting the former but rarely respecting the latter. In his stern wrath, Jehovah himself violates the sixth commandment by ordering the death of nonbelievers and others.

The Japanese philosopher Takeshi Umehara points this out and asks which is more reasonable: a religion that countenances taking human life, such as Christianity, or one that condemns it, like Buddhism? In spite of such exceptional figures as St Francis of Assisi, I find Mr Umehara's inferences about the relative reasonableness of the two religions' approaches to life convincing. Instead of the decalogue – the foundation of Western social ethics – the compassionate Buddhist view of life will be far more efficacious in establishing respect for the dignity of life throughout the world in the years to come.

The Nature of the Sacred

IKEDA: Diverse interpretations of the nature of the sacred sharply distinguish Buddhism from the Judaeo-Christian religions and Islam. For Buddhism, the most precious of all things is the Buddha nature (or Buddha life) inherent in every sentient being. The pricelessness of the inner Buddha nature is heroically symbolized by the Bodhisattvas from the Earth, described as rising from within the Earth in chapter 15 of the Lotus Sutra, the essence of Mahayana teachings.

For Christians and Muslims, on the other hand, the holiest of all things is a supernatural god dominating humanity from remote regions. The idea of God has undergone many transmutations throughout theological history. Nonetheless, people who, like Leo Tolstoy, have attempted to interpret Him as the 'god within' have always been rejected as heretics.

I believe our ability to find solutions to the problems facing humanity today will be greatly influenced by whether we regard the sacred entity as exterior and transcendent or interior and immanent.

GALTUNG: I could not agree more. I consider the transcendent-immanent distinction you mention absolutely essential. As you say, the Buddha nature (or Buddha life) inherent in every sentient being is the Buddhist formulation of immanence; Thou 'who art in Heaven' is the Christian formulation of the transcendence of both the Father and Christ ascended.

The distinction has many ramifications, of which I shall discuss only one. In several instances, Jesus says that whatever you have done unto one of my brethren you have also done unto me. (The positive version of this formula is found in Matthew XXV:40; its negative version in Matthew XXV:45.) If the act in question is evil, then the wrong is regarded as having been committed against both the direct victim and the authority 'up there' in heaven. Today, in the Western world, the political state is the secular successor to the transcendent authority of God. For instance, crimes are often called crimes against the state or against the people (once they were called crimes against the crown). The relation between the wrongdoer and the victim has been replaced with a relation between the criminal and the state, which adjudicates, sentences and punishes. By this I mean that both the victim and compassion vanish, whereas fascination with the wrongdoer and the court process persist.

In contrast, Buddhism interprets the wrongdoer and the victim as sharers of bad karma that must be jointly improved through the inner dialogue of meditation on the event, through outer dialogue between perpetrator and victim, and through right and diligent striving. The Buddhist approach brings the two parties together and could lead to the development of a less vertical social order than the one we know today. But if the Western approach can be accused of assigning guilt too asymmetrically – 100 per cent on one party only – the Buddhist view may be reprehensible for too much symmetry in this connection. There may be room for both views together.

Tolerance

IKEDA: Few religions have experienced such bloody contention over orthodoxy and heresy as Christianity. Yet in the twentieth century, perhaps inspired by regrets over the past, Christians in many parts of the world have sponsored an ecumenical movement. The idea of religious tolerance first gained significance after the Reformation. In more recent times, reflection on the bloodshed religions – and not Christianity alone – cause has stimulated conscientious people to devote increased attention to the matter.

Today the question of tolerance is becoming more pressing as we witness repeated examples of strife sparked by religious differences. Even India – the land of Hinduism, whose followers pride themselves on tolerance, and of Gandhi and his philosophy of nonviolence – is the scene of frequent acts of religion-related terrorism.

We must, of course, strive for greater tolerance. But we must also try to determine the kind of tolerance that best serves global pacific aims.

Sometimes agreements concluded between religious organizations in the name of tolerance are ineffectual because they are superficial. They amount to 'strange bedfellows' – sleeping in the same bed but dreaming different dreams, as the Japanese proverb has it. Ecumenical movements led by parties whose true – though frequently unstated – intentions diverge sharply can amount to no more than public-relations attempts to advance individual interests at the expense of the general good.

GALTUNG: Basically, dialogue must take place, but perhaps not so much between or among as within religions. Again, the inner dialogue is the precondition. Each religion faces its own internal debates: within the Catholic church, for instance, some are challenging the justness of war doctrines and the suitability of using nuclear arms in any war at all, no matter how just. As a starter they may discuss whether 'just slavery', 'just colonialism' and 'just patriarchy' make sense. Fundamentally, all these debates resolve into the distinction between the hard and soft religions that we have already mentioned. Hard religions insist that, as the heir to His divinity, the state enjoys the rights of a very vengeful, jealous God. Soft religions concentrate on the sacredness of life, including the lives of evildoers. It is therefore usual for defenders of the use of nuclear weapons to be in favor of capital punishment as well. Adherents of the soft versions of religions equate the two kinds of taking life.

Abortion too is undeniably a way of taking life. It may be that pro-life groups who are also pro-nuclear arms and capital punishment are really primarily concerned with preserving the state monopoly on institutionalized violence by forbidding women – or any non-state-authorized party – to challenge that authority. It may be equally true that pro-choice groups are more interested in breaking the state monopoly than in killing babies. Nonetheless, abortion, like violent defense or revolution, is a human capitulation that must never be legitimized, even as a last resort. It is always to be deplored.

To return to religious tolerance, I believe that all soft religionists – they are numerous and do not differ sharply among themselves because they share the assumption of immanence – should join together. Then, after essentially inter-religion dialogues have been conducted, they should invite the hard religionists to join them in inner dialogues. In our shrinking world, there are good reasons to be optimistic about this process.

Buddhism: Merits and Demerits

IKEDA: In your book, *Buddhism: A Quest for Unity and Peace*, you call Buddhism the system of faith best suited to the creation of peace and attribute to it 20 merits (including the absence of a permanent self, nonviolence, compassion, togetherness, diversity and the philosophy of the middle way) and six demerits. Revitalization of Buddhism necessitates recognizing and correcting its faults. That is why I should like to take a close look at the failings you point out.

First, you note that Buddhist toleration tends to extend even to extremely violent organizations such as nationalist militarists. Second, you believe that Buddhism acquiesces tacitly and too readily in economic structural violence. Third, you point out that

the Buddhist clergy frequently form closed groups isolated from
society and, fourth, that they sometimes ingratiate themselves with
authorities promising financial or other advantages. You add, fifth,
that its fatalistic outlook inclines Buddhism to accept defeat and,
sixth, that it occasionally becomes ritualistic and ostentatious.
Similar criticisms are frequently leveled at Christianity too.

All these tendencies emerge when Buddhism neglects its fundamental role as a religion for the people and, in isolation from the
masses, subjugates itself to political or religious authorities. Owing
to the immanent nature of the Law (*dharma*), to overcome its
failings Buddhism must undergo a ceaseless process of renaissance
resulting from searching self-examination.

GALTUNG: When it submits to political authorities who appropriate and begin exerting control over religious affairs, Buddhism too
easily declines into the six demerits. (Of course, the list could be
either expanded or abbreviated.) It is vital to remember that
Buddhism was and is a protest movement against both political and
religious authorities. It is profoundly revolutionary, though not in
the external Marxist sense. Buddhism emphasizes the inner
revolution. But the inner revolution must find external, as well as
internal, expression. Remaining contentedly in a little *sangha*, or
in private enlightenment, for life and constantly meditating,
withdrawn from the world, do not make a good Buddhist.

The very idea of Buddhism as a state religion is a contradiction
in terms. Buddhism can remain true to the inspiration of
Shakyamuni's philosophy only as long as it refuses to withdraw into
exclusivism and retains its independence, allowing diverse interpretations and schools to blossom in symbiotic relationship.
Diversity of this kind limits organizational scale.

IKEDA: As you imply, maintaining proper relations with political
authorities is of maximum importance in helping Buddhism
overcome its shortcomings. This is an issue to which I have devoted
a great deal of thought ever since I first came into contact with the
Buddhism of the great Japanese leader Nichiren Daishonin. One
of the conclusions I have reached is that failure to consider relations
with authorities honestly has led Buddhist tolerance to be extended
even to the acceptance of political violence.

I am further convinced that the teachings and religious practice
of Nichiren Daishonin alone propose penetrating solutions to this
problem. You say that Buddhism is a protest movement against
both political and religious authority. I believe that Nichiren
Daishonin is the only person in the history of Buddhism to have
given that protest both philosophical and behavioral form.

Consistently remonstrating with politicians in order to enlighten them, Nichiren Daishonin did not reject political authority outright. On the other hand, he was never blindly obedient to it. True to his responsibility as a religious leader, he fearlessly condemned and attempted to have corrected all political errors and injustices that threatened the happiness of the ordinary people.

A number of factors make remonstrations like his possible. One is a combination of inner independence, strength and magnanimity. Only the person who is truly enlightened to supreme inner values realizes that political values are only relative, not absolute. When political persecution confronted him, Nichiren Daishonin was able to say, 'Since I have been born in the ruler's domain, I must follow him in my actions. But I need not follow him in the beliefs of my heart' (*The Major Writings of Nichiren Daishonin*, vol. 2, p. 171). In spite of all the pressure they exerted on him, the Japanese political authorities could never touch the Daishonin's inner enlightenment. (He referred to his own innermost self as the richest person in all Japan.)

As if to underscore the merely relative importance of political power, he admonished his disciples not to fear persecution from the authorities, whom he described as the 'rulers of this little island country'. On the other hand, he accurately perceived that the true, inner Law promises to save everyone and said that prophetic remonstrations against people in political power in the present world cast no doubt on their future salvation. In short, his criticism of political authorities amounted to attempts to enlighten the misguided and therefore were external expressions of the Daishonin's inner state of enlightenment. This strikes me as an illustration of what you refer to as giving external expression to the internal revolution.

Another problem that Buddhism must face is that of abandoning the monastic tradition in favor of becoming a religion open to the masses of the people. Adherents of monastic isolationism seek their own private enlightenment to inner values but are in no position to effect political changes through counsel and guidance. Only Buddhists who share the life of the masses are able to perform this service.

GALTUNG: Ernst Schumacher (1911–77) was correct when in his book *Small is Beautiful* he spoke of 'Buddhist economics' as emphasizing respect for life, work as self-realization, social usefulness and forming networks with others. All of these things are easier to accomplish in small units.

Interestingly, today business managers are discovering the superiority of small units. While it may look impressive, the big national or transnational corporation is actually wasteful. Human beings work better in smaller units of, say, 20 to 30 people who know and relate to each other than they do in pyramidal structures of hundreds or thousands presided over by a chief executive officer, the CEO. The big structure may survive for coordination purposes. Some of the 'big' is necessary, but in other contexts it will give way to small, autonomous units. This is the way of Buddhism, which, though lacking a pope or a Vatican of its own, is nonetheless coherent. It is a question of both-and instead of either-or.

IKEDA: Undeniably, attention to small autonomous units is essential if we are to overcome the failings of vast, over-managed modern society. But the task is too complicated to be reduced to a simple choice between large and small. I agree that, in terms of economic efficiency, the enormous, modern, pyramidal organization has almost reached its limit. The tendency either to ignore or to under-estimate the importance of the individual economic life has brought this situation about. Individuals clearly cannot manifest their abilities fully in oversized organizations targeted solely at specific economic goals. It may be symptomatic of a realization of this impos-sibility that, according to recent surveys, young Japanese lay greater stress on meaningfulness than on salary in selecting their careers.

The fundamental merits of small organizations must be used to the full. Still, large groups have their merits. The important issue is not size but focus on humanity and willingness to allow all members of the organization to play visible roles in its operations.

Large conglomerates can be composed of small organizations linked together in such a way as to promote greater openness and fluidity. They can, metaphorically speaking, be the body of water in which the smaller fry – the small groups – flourish. As long as they exist to serve their constituent elements, large organizations have ample significance for the future.

Nor have Buddhists always limited themselves to small organi-zations. It is true that during Shakyamuni's lifetime the order was a small group of people engaged in religious discipline. But their ultimate goal was to carry the teachings to the whole world; that is, to form the universal *sangha*. Furthermore, mutual exchange and a sense of belonging to a greater body were stimulated by the custom of making facilities in all regions available to traveling monks from all other areas. A similar cultivation of mutual exchanges would benefit large organizations today.

GALTUNG: The weakness apparent in smallness of scale conceals great strength. An inevitable consequence of organizational bigness is isolation from society; and this is partly responsible for the third of the six demerits to which Buddhism is susceptible. Isolated from the people and from the old *bhikkhu*, or monastic, tradition, the clergy become administrators and organizers. To an extent, because of a predilection for retreat and emphasis on withdrawal, meditation and the very small *sangha*, isolation is built into Buddhism. It is more noticeable in the Hinayana than in the Mahayana tradition. Social participation, including participation in political parties, can counteract both kinds of isolationism. In the case of political parties, however, the actual meaning of Buddhist politics must be thoroughly discussed and understood.

The environmentalist, so-called Green, parties that, in spite of difficulties and a degree of sectarianism, are springing up all over the world today resemble the Buddhist tradition but lack the ethos and the inner guidance informed by millennia of experience.

IKEDA: In the past, in both the Hinayana and Mahayana traditions, members of the *sangha* tended to isolate themselves from ordinary society because they required a tranquil environment in which to live regulated lives, engrossed in their inner beings. But later, owing to the altruistic nature of their beliefs and discipline, Mahayanists came to focus their energies outward, on society and its well-being.

The Buddhism of Nichiren Daishonin meticulously evolved doctrines and disciplines that, in keeping with the Mahayana tradition, develop the altruistic Bodhisattva spirit even more assiduously among lay believers than among the clergy. Symbolic of this tendency is an instance in which Nichiren Daishonin counseled a lay believer against taking monastic vows because life in ordinary society is the true essence of the Buddhist Law. The outward orientation of this approach evolves logically from the Lotus Sutra teaching of the possibility of all sentient beings attaining Buddhahood.

Equating life in ordinary society with the Buddha Law results from emphasizing those ideas and attitudes that, emerging from within the human being, affect the outside world. Instead of stressing passive self-engrossment, the Buddhism of Nichiren Daishonin – the Buddhism for people living now, in the Latter Day of the Law – stresses externally projected expressions of the inner self. Inwardly oriented Buddhism idealizes isolation from society. Buddhism that stresses the external expression of the inner self, on the other hand, equates the Buddha Law with life in actual society. In different terms, life within society provides contributory causes (*en*[*] in Japanese, or *prataya* in Sanskrit) for outward expressions

---

[*] *En*: Relation, sometimes translated as external cause. The auxiliary cause, or external stimulus, which helps an internal cause produce its effect. Relation is not the environment itself but the function relating life to its environment. (From *A Dictionary of Buddhist Terms and Concepts*.)

of the inner self. This amounts to a practical manifestation of the fundamental Buddhist doctrine of production by causation (*engiron*: dependent origination, the Buddhist doctrine of the interdependence of all things).

You say the environmentalist Green groups resemble Buddhism, except for their lack of ethos. The environmentalists' emphasis on the global chain of life and the solidarity of all phenomena approximates the Buddhist doctrine of production by causation. If, as you say, they lack ethos, it is of course due in part to lack of experience and probably to the incompleteness of their interpretation of the doctrine of production by causation, which, for them, stops at the level of perception.

The Buddhism of Nichiren Daishonin puts that doctrine to work on the level of human practice and daily life. It transcends the dimension on which all phenomena are perceived as interrelated and reveals the dynamism of the universal life on which all interrelations depend. To formulate one's own ethos of the doctrine of production by causation – what I call the ethos of symbiosis – it is essential to discover that dynamism within one's own individual life.

GALTUNG: My fourth point is this: autonomy tends to disappear when funds are provided by political authorities – especially if they are the only source of funding. As the English say, 'He who pays the piper, calls the tune.' Buddhism may choose one or both of two paths. It may have its own independent financial sources; perhaps contributions from members or small businesses. Or it may be very frugal. It cannot, however, be paid and maintained from the outside. Such a situation would stimulate only subservience in the hope of maintaining monetary support at its current level or getting more.

IKEDA: In the past, with a few exceptions, all Japanese Buddhist groups have kowtowed to the political authorities that protected them. In the Edo period (1615–1867), which witnessed the ultimate degradation of Japanese Buddhism, Buddhist sects were all agencies of thought-control for the immensely powerful Tokugawa shogunate. Many of them are in grave difficulties today precisely because of their inability to break with this past.

I agree with you that, without autonomy – the independence to say no to political authorities on all things, even sources of revenue – religions grow decadent and lose the spiritual drive that motivated their founders.

Jesus said render unto Caesar the things that are Caesar's and unto God the things that are God's. As this teaching implies it must, the Christian church has sometimes managed to maintain independence from and even to oppose political authority. Such religious autonomy is not without its faults, one of which is the tendency for the religion itself to assume a mantle of authority. The Christian church did precisely this when, assuming the role of sole intermediary between humanity and God, it demanded allegiance that not infrequently clashed with the secular allegiances.

A religious order can attain full autonomy only by relying entirely on the masses. Taking the side of the people in all conflicts must be its ironclad rule. Doctrinally and practically, a truly autonomous religion must exist for the sake of people.

Soka Gakkai International is founded on the Buddhism of Nichiren Daishonin, which exists solely for the sake of the people. It therefore strives tirelessly for self-purification in the original spirit of our founder. Spontaneous faith and efforts to carry Nichiren Daishonin's teachings to as many people as possible constitute the basis of all our practical actions. We strive to eliminate authoritarianism and emphasize serving the needs of our members.

GALTUNG: Fatalism, the fifth on my list of demerits, is stronger in the Hinayana tradition. The Lord Buddha cannot be interpreted as having said that life must always consist of dissatisfaction and suffering (*dukkha*). Suffering is, of course, the first of the Four Noble Truths[*]. But the remaining three explain how to overcome *dukkha* and approach happiness (*sukha*). Living in a way that satisfies family and others' needs without luxury makes perfectly good sense. I am fond of such good things as automobiles and computers but can live without them. Losing the ability to do without makes people the victims of craving. In this connection, we Norwegians are aided by our innate fondness for simplicity, primitive mountain huts and proximity to nature. We believe vacations should be liberating. That is why our idea of a vacation is seeking simplicity close to or in the world of nature, camping and living in a hut or a tent, and not spending days or weeks in a luxurious hotel in a famous city. The Buddhist social order can be dynamic – economically dynamic too. Indulging in suffering as an inevitability is no proof of being a true Buddhist. The important task is to overcome suffering by living according to the other three of the Four Noble Truths, particularly the third in the form of the Eightfold Path[†].

---

[*] Four Noble Truths: The truths of suffering, the origin of suffering, the cessation of suffering and the path to the cessation of suffering. A fundamental doctrine of Buddhism clarifying the cause of suffering and the way of emancipation. (From *A Dictionary of Buddhist Terms and Concepts*.)

[†] Eightfold Path: An early teaching of Buddhism setting forth the principles to be observed in order to attain emancipation. They are: (1) right views, (2) right thinking, (3) right speech, (4) right action, (5) right way of life, (6) right endeavor, (7) right mindfulness and (8) right meditation. In Shakyamuni's teaching, the Eightfold Path is regarded as the path to the cessation of suffering. (From *A Dictionary of Buddhist Terms and Concepts*.)

These guidelines, which embody myriads of years of experience in the great chain of dependent co-arising (*paticca samuppada*) are difficult to abide by: we all have our difficulties. Still, we can and must try. As Goethe says in *Faust*, 'Wer strebend sich bemüht, den können wir erlösen' ('We can redeem him who strives').

Actually, fatalism is anti-Buddhist. Had Shakyamuni been a fatalist, he would never have struggled to share his liberating, empowering insights with others.

IKEDA: Certainly Shakyamuni taught not resignation to, but triumph over suffering. Identifying human life with suffering breeds pessimism. Undeniably this is the source of Hinayanist fatalism.

Perhaps distinctly Indian characteristics prompted Shakyamuni to give suffering a conspicuous position among the noble truths. Indian teachings claim that human beings must accept life as predetermined and must strive to break free of the eternal cycle of endless reincarnations to find release from rebirth. The Truth of Suffering is easy to understand in the light of this philosophy.

Certain elements in his own life suggest that Shakyamuni himself found it impossible to shake off Indian approaches to matters of this kind. For example, it is said that, after his enlightenment, he considered his teaching too difficult to teach to others. He therefore prepared to enter Nirvana at once, but the god Brahma convinced him to alter his plans and teach. Had he remained content with his own enlightenment and entered Nirvana without teaching, Shakyamuni would have remained at the Pratyekabuddha level of one who finds enlightenment on his own and for himself alone; that is, he would never have attained full Buddhahood. I suspect that Shakyamuni's hesitation reflects the traditional Indian dislike of the prospect of reincarnation.

Fatalism becomes apparent in Shakyamuni in his late years, especially in his attitude toward the annihilation of his own Shakya tribe at the hands of the king of Kosala. When told of this, Shakyamuni is said only to have remarked that annihilation was the unavoidable karmic retribution for the Shakyas' acts in previous existences. While it is true that this tradition may have a strong Hinayanist coloring, it nonetheless suggests that Shakyamuni was not entirely free of Indian fatalism.

In its widest definition, Buddhism includes not merely Indian but also Chinese and Japanese characteristics. Although I recognize the profundity of the observations embodied in them, the Four Noble Truths reflect an exclusively Indian approach. In order to revitalize Buddhism as a religion for the whole world today, we must plumb its essentials, freed of all traces of strictly regional coloration.

We should reinterpret the Four Noble Truths and uncover the wisdom that is their consistent essence: that is, birth, aging, illness

and death are suffering; the cause of suffering is delusion; eliminating delusion is eliminating suffering; and the way to eliminate
delusion is set forth in the Eightfold Righteous Path of conduct.

Mahayana Buddhism explores the depths of this wisdom. The
Lotus Sutra reveals Buddha wisdom as inherent in all sentient beings.
Nichiren Daishonin explains how the so-called Three Ways – the
cycle of delusions, acts karmically determined by delusion, and
suffering arising from those acts – are converted into the Three
Virtues*. These merits constitute the inherent Buddha nature,
which generates the wisdom of enlightenment, which in turn brings
liberation from suffering. As you can see, this teaching is free of
the least trace of fatalism.

GALTUNG: Almost inevitably, ritualism, the sixth demerit, approaches
the status of a social law. Obsessed with exterior behavioral forms
such as temple attendance and certain gestures (for example, the
gassho hand position with palms joined), people can lose sight of
inner meanings. Once again speaking personally, while in Hawaii
I sometimes go to a Korean Buddhist temple early in the morning,
often with my beloved friend Glenn Paige, who is a Buddhist, too.
While there, I sometimes become so absorbed in the solitude and
splendor of the place that I forget deeper, spiritual considerations.
We can all try to combat such tendencies in ourselves. Without
blaming others, we must revitalize the Buddha nature within us.
We must never capitulate. For me, inner dialogue as a form of
meditation is so useful that I can almost stage inner dramas in which
I play my various inclinations against each other without suppres-
sion, listening to them and gently guiding the dialogue toward
Buddhist truths.

IKEDA: I agree that combating ritualism requires an inner struggle.
In an address I once delivered at Harvard University, I said that
religions must subordinate the institutional to the personal. I
pointed out how most religions fall into the trap of allowing external
powers, like the power of ritual, to suppress such inner-generated
power as the force of faith. The internal struggle assumes added
importance when weak inner-generated powers are confronted by
powerful organizations. This occurs in many aspects of life.

---

*Three Virtues: The three virtues of the property of the Law (Sanskrit *dharmakaya*,
Japanese *hosshin*), wisdom (*prajna*, *hannya*) and emancipation or freedom (*vimukti*,
gedatsu) which a Buddha possesses. The property of the Law is the truth which the
Buddha has realized, or the true entity of life; wisdom is the capacity to realize this
truth; and emancipation is the state of being free from the sufferings of birth and
death. These three also correspond respectively to the three bodies, or properties,
of the Buddha: the property of the law, the property of wisdom and the property
of action. (From *A Dictionary of Buddhist Terms and Concepts*.)

The individual can be expected to demonstrate greater originality than the organization. As the philosopher Thomas Samuel Kuhn says, individual creative discoveries always bring about scientific revolutions. The same is true in the case of religion. It was Martin Luther's faith that breached the authority of a corrupt church. The inner struggle prepares the way for the manifestation of inwardly-generated and outwardly-oriented strength and activity.

GALTUNG: The inner dialogue promotes this manifestation by giving internal voice to both pro and con arguments. For this reason, I have come to consider my inner freedom of speech equally as important as the celebrated social outer version. We must examine our tacit assumptions and attitudes not by denying their existence, but by exposing them in the hope of understanding them. At dialogue time, many people exercise an inner dictatorship over themselves. Instead of doing this, they ought to reexamine the politics of their own minds and become less afraid of inner opposition.

A New, Global Mahayana

IKEDA: Western intellectuals have often criticized Buddhism. Henri Bergson was dissatisfied with what he considered its lack of élan, or the energy to enable it to confront social reality. The British philosopher Alfred North Whitehead (1861–1947), too, voiced dissatisfaction with Buddhism for being limited to fruitless, passive meditation. But with the emergence of New Age Science in the 1970s, Westerners began regarding Oriental philosophies, including Buddhism, more positively. To an extent, the unflatteringly revealing light shed on its greed and destructive aspects by increased awareness of the nuclear threat and environmental pollution awakened many people to the limitations of Western individualism.

As you yourself have noticed, the shortcomings and good points of Buddhism are often two sides of the same coin. The doctrine of the absence of a persisting self – at the top of your positive list – can elevate and purify excessive occidental individualism, to which it is of course antipodean. But if taken to mean total self-negation and if carried to its logical extreme, it can lead people – and often has led Hinayanists – to abnegate the vital energy that engenders desires. Such an approach inevitably invites nihilism. (Perhaps this is the kind of thing that Bergson and Whitehead found distasteful.)

Because of its shortcomings, Buddhism must continue striving for further self-revival and renewal. To this end, we must generate a new Mahayana movement open to the entire world. During its

2,500 years of history, Buddhism has experienced numerous revivals, all of which aimed to break away from the domination of clerical factions and recover the pristine radiance of the faith. All these movements have consistently been guided by unwavering determination to give Buddhism back to the people.

You have called the Soka Gakkai International movement an exemplary and stimulating exception to the Buddhist generality. In the face of current global problems, Buddhism must divest itself of established, traditional frameworks. We realize this and value your thoughts on a revitalized, global Mahayana movement.

GALTUNG: Once, back in the old communist days, a Buddhist from Mongolia said something that greatly impressed me: 'Let us not make too much of Hinayana and Mahayana. As a Buddhist, I believe in Buddhayana.' His statement may seem simple, even simplistic. But there is something in what he said. Both Hinayana and Mahayana have their strong and weak points. If the Hinayanists are prone to become too private, withdrawn and fatalistic – even nihilistic – the Mahayanists sometimes succumb to the temptation of identifying any great vehicle at all – even world-market automobile manufacturers, if the play on words may be forgiven – with Buddhism.

One aspect of Mahayana teachings, however, is quintessentially Buddhist: universal solidarity with all forms of life, not only in the present but also in the past and future. The Western tendency is to view the past as dead and gone. Buddhism connects all life, past, present and future, in a dependent co-arising. The theory of causality at the heart of Buddhism is much closer to Aristotle's complex view of causality than is the reductionist Western notion today of efficient causes only. As the author Joanna Macy points out in her excellent book on the subject, Buddhism is never limited to one god, one prophet and one scripture.

In concrete terms, this means synchronic solidarity with all present life, diachronic solidarity with future life and solidarity with the life-struggles of the past. Although care to avoid the many pitfalls lying in the way must be exercised, it is possible to fit into this formula the struggle for development and a wholesome environment and efforts to create a better United Nations.

Development must concentrate on decreasing *dukkha*, or suffering. Translated into Western jargon, this means satisfying basic human needs for everyone, beginning of course with the neediest; that is, the people with the greatest amount of *dukkha* to decrease. This is certainly not synonymous with economic growth, as it is understood today. The dimension that really matters is the *dukkha–sukha* (suffering–happiness) ratio. As is often pointed out,

the gross national product is a very inadequate gauge of this
dimension.

Entailing much more than things that can be satisfied purely economically, minimal human basic needs include not only a certain
level of material well-being, but also a reason to live, an identity
and the freedom to move and to choose physically and mentally.
The most basic need of all is the need to live, to survive, individually or collectively, as a person, a family, a clan, a nation or a species.

The needs of nonhuman nature, too, must be taken into consideration. Buddhism considers humanity part of the Great Chain
of Living. Certainly survival means as much to plants and other
animals – at least to species – as it does to human beings. A
minimum level of well-being, including proper shares of available
sunlight, water and nutrients, is essential to them. Perhaps nonhuman
life experiences a kind of happiness or *sukha* in a modicum of
freedom or self-realization, in the form of unfolding, as seeds do.
Buddhism elegantly employs a single umbrella to cover both the
development and the environment problematiques. It might be
objected that decreasing *dukkha* does not necessarily mean increasing
sukha. Surely being truly happy means desiring and having a little
more than the satisfaction of minimal needs. But the additional
necessary for happiness is better if it comes in nonmaterial forms.
People really engaged in creative work, such as the artist or the
researcher, are too absorbed in what they are doing to have time
to indulge in material possessions. The creative act gives their lives
meaning. Spiritual growth is a still more inclusive category than
creativity. There must be some latitude between Gandhi's extremes
of 'enough for everybody's needs' and 'not enough for everybody's
greed'. We do not have to live at the bare subsistence level, but we
do have to be careful.

How we create our wealth is of the greatest importance. We must
exploit neither other human beings nor the natural environment.
At its worst, exploitation means taking so much away that the
exploited become incapable of reproducing and die out.

As has already been mentioned, I consider the second of the
Buddhist Five Precepts (*pancha silani*: not to take life, not to take
what is not given, not to commit adultery, not to tell lies and not
to drink intoxicants) completely adequate in connection with this
point. The precept exhorts us not merely not to steal, but also not
to take what is neither given nor freely offered. Of course, stealing
is part of this broader category. But so is establishing an economic
system according to which the top 10 per cent of the population
pockets 90 per cent of the value produced. The remaining 90 per
cent of the population would never authorize such a thing, for various
reasons – first of all because they are never asked about it. Such a
disproportionate share is certainly never freely offered to the rich

minority. Similarly, slave-owners are not accused of stealing when they take what they want – for instance, freedom – from their slaves. Their crime, however, is too big to be covered by the term 'theft'. Moreover, economic exploitation and slavery have been seen as a part of the normal operation of the social structure.

Interestingly, Buddhist thought can also easily accommodate three major strands of modern Western thought – liberal emphasis on freedom to develop, Marxist emphasis on equity and justice and rejection of exploitation, and the more recent ecological emphasis on the natural environment. Buddhism is remarkable because it focuses not on one of these elements, but on all three.

An improved United Nations – or, to use a broader formulation, a central world governance – must be coordinated with something along the lines of what you call a revitalized global Mahayana 'open to the world'. It and the world governance must be just as open to misbehaving states and nations as to those that conduct themselves properly. The misbehaving must not be excluded, because they are more in need than anyone else of a sense of belonging and of participating in the common effort toward fulfillment. The Buddhist does not discredit malefactors as guilty but tries to understand the origin of their misbehavior and then seeks to change the bad karma making them behave as they do.

Your comment on the numerous revivals that have occurred throughout the history of Buddhism inspires me. Perhaps the quality of a religion can be measured by the number of times it has been able to revive itself and counter the widespread tendency toward ritualization and routine. Maybe the major danger is less domination by clerical elements and appropriation at the hands of political authorities than self-divorce from compassion (*karuna*), the first of the *pancha silani*.

The compassionate empathize with the sufferings of others. At one time or another, most of us experience the suffering of other people as if it were our own. We can even share the suffering of pain-inflicters and of nonhuman nature. We must expand and build on those occasional feelings, even at the risk of increasing our own *dukkha*. Reward in the form of improved karma for both parties comes when we realize that we can relieve the pain of others.

I should like to summarize my thoughts on this topic with some concrete proposals about development and the environment in what I interpret as the Buddhist spirit:

1. The size of human settlements should be greatly reduced, preferably to communities of no more than 5,000 inhabitants living closer to nature and to each other.

2. The inhabitants of these settlements should attempt to be self-sufficient in terms of foodstuffs, clothing, housing and building materials, education, and health and social care for the young, the old, the sick, and the handicapped. To make this self-sufficiency sustainable (that is, reproducible or, more simply, lasting) requires three-dimensional agriculture, hydroponics, and energy conversion by means of biomass, wind, waves and thermal and solar power.

3. Nonmaterial, spiritual production, distribution and consumption must be stimulated. Commercialism and capitalism notwithstanding, interesting things are going on today in the many communities in the world that make their livelihoods from art galleries, museums, festivals, seminars and conferences. Although in modern forms it is less dogmatic, devotion to such undertakings recalls medieval dedication to monasteries and cathedrals. More of the economic surplus should go to cultural and spiritual concerns and less to an economic growth that is unsustainable anyway.

4. Excellent collective transportation and communications systems must connect the communities. They should remain close to each other and to nature, but people must be free to alter their places of residence and lifestyles to suit their preferences.

IKEDA: As a Buddhist, I am greatly encouraged by the way you employ basic Buddhist doctrines – causal origination, suffering, the Five Precepts and so on – to shed light on the modern complex of problems, including global solidarity, conditions for development and environmental issues. I have given a great deal of consideration to the matter for some years and agree completely with you that the doctrine of causal origination can serve as a basis for global solidarity.

But for it to do so, it must be reexamined. In the past, causal origination has been negatively interpreted in connection with such other doctrines as the impermanence of all things and the non-substantiality of the self. Since all things arise from causes, they are in themselves ephemeral and without substance.

I prefer to take a more positive view of the doctrine, because I consider the negative one meaningful only in the Indian social society of Shakyamuni's day, when authoritarian and formalized Brahmanism had stifled creative energy. To combat the greed and confusion permeating this debilitated society, it was essential to approach causality negatively – in a nihilistic fashion – and to relate it to the doctrines of impermanence and nonsubstantiality.

According to the German philospher Friedrich Nietzsche (1844–1900), there are two kinds of nihilism: active and passive. Passive nihilism he describes as a decline or recession of spiritual power. He considers active nihilism, on the other hand, to be a sign of spiritual ascent. In Nietzsche's view, active nihilism is oriented toward new creative theses, or what he calls the will to power.

Indicative of the prevalence of passive nihilism in the India of Shakyamuni's day is the way in which people allowed the theory of the endless cycle of reincarnations to breed resignation about the present life and, incidentally, to help reinforce the caste system. Shakyamuni's doctrines of impermanence and the nonsubstantiality of the self functioned in the same way as Nietzsche's active nihilism in that they aimed to rectify a prevailing passive, negative nihilism. Consequently, like his active nihilism, these two doctrines are oriented toward the creation of new value-theses.

Even if they are only milestones along the way, the doctrines of impermanence and the nonsubstantiality of the self indicate the way to enlightenment. In Mahayana terms, these teachings are means (*upaya*) of guiding sentient beings to the truth. After reaching the end of this phase of the journey, the enlightened being returns to his or her sphere of existence to apply this enlightenment to the creation of new values. Enlightenment makes creating new values possible. As the doctrine of causal origination explains, all things are interrelated. For the sake of creating new values, therefore, the enlightened being has limitless possibilities at his or her disposal.

In a passage reminiscent of the Buddhist idea of causal origination, Nietzsche says that links in the chain of being are inherent in the individual. He adds that categories are no more than abstractions of the diversity of the whole chain and the similarity of its parts. If we identify the idea of causal origination and its resultant universal interrelatedness with Nietzsche's belief that the individual and the chain of being are one, it seems possible to equate his will oriented toward the creation of new value-theses with the Buddhist idea of the enlightened will with limitless creative possibilities at its disposal. (Interestingly, the German word for power, *Macht*, derives from the same root as the word for possibility, *Möglichkeit*.)

The concepts of impermanence and the nonsubstantiality of the self seem to suggest equating enlightenment and self-extinction. In this way they actually reinforce the very passive nihilism that Shakyamuni was eager to overcome. Hinayana Buddhism stresses these two concepts. Therefore, since it emphasizes self-enlightenment for its own sake, Hinayana goes no further than the shallow idea of enlightenment attained as a result of self-extinction. It ignores the responsibility of the enlightened being to create new values. In contrast, Mahayana Buddhism places maximum emphasis on value-creation by the enlightened for the sake of the achievement of the ultimate goal: enlightenment for all sentient beings.

In order for it to serve as a basis for global solidarity, the doctrine of causal origination must be isolated from association with the teachings of impermanence and the nonsubstantial self and re-interpreted in the context of value-creation or, to borrow Nietzsche's terminology, new value-theses.

To this end, the doctrine must be recognized as a guideline for thought and behavior. It must be seen as a program for cultivating people ready to accept diverse possibilities and capable of drawing on the limitless generative power of the world of causal origination – or what I call the power of internally-generated, outwardly-oriented values.

The doctrine of causal origination amounts to an ethos of symbiosis – an ethos that ought to be shared by all peoples. In an address delivered to the Chinese Academy of Social Sciences, I defined the ethos of symbiosis as 'a psychological tendency to favor harmony over opposition, unity over division, "we" over "I"; a belief that human beings should live together harmoniously with each other and with nature, support each other and flourish together'. Only when it is seen by all to be such an ethos will the doctrine of causal origination have the power to serve effectively as a basis for global solidarity.

The ethos of symbiosis is a force for harmonious and peaceful revolution. In contrast, though oriented toward new value-theses, Nietzsche's active nihilism inevitably has destruction – often violent destruction – as its premise. Only the ethos of symbiosis can ensure absolutely nondestructive value-creation.

During the late 1960s and the early 1970s, students all over the world manifested active nihilism by rejecting all modern values. Their efforts began and ended in destruction and division. Nietzsche himself characterized the nihilist process as destruction brought on by destruction. The impulse to self-destruction generates destructive acts. Often the self depends on generally accepted value-criteria. When they rejected those criteria, the students were in effect rejecting at least part of their selves. Self-rejection is in a very real sense self-destruction. Social nihilism is restricted to external and externally imposed values. Self-enlightenment to one's own inherent values can halt or reverse the destructive process.

Certainly the most important and fundamental of inner values is the dignity of life. Since all things originate from causes, all things are mutually interdependent; and each individual life-element is a recapitulation of all others. The dignity of life derives from the union of its inextricably intertwined aspects.

Nichiren Daishonin identified compassion and the Buddha nature as the central feature of the world governed by causal origination and pointed out their effects on such phenomena as earth, water, fire, wind and air. In a poetic fashion, he said that the contributory (as distinct from direct) causes of spring wind and rain make plants bloom, whereas the contributory cause of autumn moonlight brings trees to fruition. Nichiren Daishonin taught that all sentient and non-sentient things in the universe are cultivated by the Buddha nature on which all things, including causal origination, depend. The Buddha nature is one with the force of life, the dignity of which must be recognized as both an internal and a universal value if the ethos of symbiosis is to become real and effective.

GALTUNG: The universal nature of these considerations is inspiring. Buddhism is a profound psychology not only of the individual mind or the collective unconscious, but of all life as well. There is no necessity to submit to the will of any Superior Being, who, as is clearly true in the cases of Judaism, Christianity and Islam, inevitably assumes the characteristics of his human creators. Buddhism's rich material for a world ethos includes a strong emphasis on nonviolence, a nonexploitative approach to the natural world and a spirit of compassion free of clever sophistry, all of which are badly needed in our deeply troubled world.

CHAPTER 5

Putting the People in Charge

Grassroots Power

IKEDA: You have said the following three elements were simultaneously operative in the revolutions that swept the Soviet Union
and East Europe: people power, primacy of politics and peaceful
policies. Citing popular reaction against both the nuclear peril and
Stalinist repression, you describe how the power of the ordinary
people profoundly influenced world leaders in East and West and
Western mass media.

You dismiss as vulgar materialism the notion that economic
factors alone stimulate popular uprisings and point out how concern
for democracy, human rights and independence incite people to
risk their lives to act on their own behalf. Stirred by emotionally
charged slogans, reminiscent of the 'We shall overcome' of the blacks
in the United States, the East Europeans reinforced my own belief
in the masses as the bedrock of history. As long as they work
together, the people can change the current of events.

We now confront the daunting problem of sustaining the popular
thrust for liberation while channeling its energy into constructive
courses. The East Europeans won a victory. Now the task is to incorporate them creatively into the current of general European
unification and the evolution of a new international order. In April
1992 Mr Gorbachev made me feel much more optimistic about
the future when he said that everything depends on the continua-
tion of the process of democratization.

GALTUNG: The two great grassroots movements of the 1980s were
those of the dissidents in the East and the peace activists in both
East and West. They were directed against the two terrors administered by the elite in each zone: Stalinism in the East and nuclearism
in both East and West. The grassroots movements won. Stalinist
regimes crumbled; and the nuclear threat was removed for the time
being from what the Americans used to call the European 'theater'.
But the politicians and others who planned a nuclear holocaust that
might have taken 500 million lives are still among us. No doubt
they are pleased that the world is now focusing attention on the
Stalinists and their successors.

It is important to remember that grassroots movements are not necessarily guaranteed either to be democratic and progressive or to work for the enhancement of life. They may of course fight for democracy; but they may also promote the success of entirely different agendas. The movements Hitler and Mussolini headed were grassroots as well. Many of the people who kill in the former Yugoslavia, too, claim grassroots motivations. Such movements are also anti-elite in that they oppose elites attempting to practice some kind of democracy (actually party-ocracy and parliament-ocracy). Hitler and Mussolini frustrated the feeble democratic attempts to confront them, with results that are all too well known.

In Japan at about the same time, grassroots movements had little effect. Deeply embedded in the Japanese tradition is a sense of being a chosen people under the protection of the Sun Goddess (Amaterasu). This 'chosenness' and the idea of the whole universe as a single house (*hakko ichi-u*) centered in Japan were used by Japanese imperialist militarists to justify expansionist policies. In the face of this tradition and the vertically-oriented society of Japan, the grassroots movements sponsored by communists, Christians and people such as Tsunesaburo Makiguchi, founder of Soka Gakkai, failed to influence the mainstream.

Grassroots movements alone cannot correct authoritarian elites; no more can democratic elites by themselves prevent authoritarian grassroots movements from achieving power. Some radiant guidelines must illumine the interplay between elites and the masses of the people. In spite of the many problems associated with them – problems that I believe can be resolved – human rights constitute one such set of guidelines. The light emitted by Buddhism and the gentler aspects of all religions constitute another. Though abstract and hardly emotionally stirring, such ecological concepts as diversity and symbiosis for the enhancement of life provide still another set of guidelines.

What happens if elites or those who overthrow elites to achieve power in their turn are not guided by rules of these kinds? Such instances might seem to justify some sort of intervention, though certainly not intervention by killing 'with all necessary means' as called for by the United Nations Security Council in the name of enforcing peace (Resolution 678 legitimizing the Second Gulf War). We need something new, something different.

The acceptable kind of international action in such cases must resemble what took place in East Europe during the 1980s. I mean the operation of the Western peace movement on East European soil: intervention by means of dialogues not only with dissidents and members of the Eastern peace movement, but also with power elites. The result was the formation of an international civil society, a kind of internationalized grassroots movement of considerable

strength. A similar spirit, by means of which international democratization tries to modify state intergovernmental and corporate
transnational powers, was at work at the United Nations Conference
on the Environment and Development (UNCED) in Rio de Janeiro
(1992) and the World Human Rights Conference in Vienna (1993)
and will be active at more rounds in the years to come. Scale, too,
is important. We need hundreds of thousands, millions, of people
capable of nonviolent intervention.

IKEDA: We need all of the masses of the peoples of the world. To
follow the royal road to peace, the masses must be strong – that
is, wise. It is dangerous to permit a handful of specialists, isolated
from the masses, to determine policies. A top-echelon elite started
and pursued the Vietnam War, which degenerated into a hopeless
morass and still symbolizes the peril of establishing policies without
the participation of the ordinary people.

The people must always play the leading role. They must be the
deciding factor. In a democratic society founded on a wise populace,
no administrative government would be able to establish diplomatic
policies that fail to reflect the popular will. One of the things that
impress me most deeply about Mr Gorbachev is the way he clung
to the idea of democratization as an expression of the will of the
people throughout the trial-and-error perestroika period. I especially
appreciate his having chosen peace as his main goal. In this
connection, I have consistently proposed that each nation form a
ministry of peace specifically and exclusively for the consideration
of peace-related problems.

If, as you say, grassroots movements had little effect in the days
of the prewar Japanese militarists, I think Soka Gakkai illustrates
the way such movements can develop and become important in
the present-day world. In the final period of World War II, Josei
Toda, the man who led Soka Gakkai to reconstruction after World
War II, was incarcerated for his struggle against the militarists and
religious organizations that pandered to them. (Interestingly,
Gandhi was in prison for the last time at about the same period.)
After Toda's release, and with the end of hostilities, our organization grew strong because it has always sided with and striven to
educate the ordinary people.

Gandhi's struggle in the name of nonviolence was a battle to make
the people strong and wise. For this reason, populism was one of
the four points I stressed in my speech at the Gandhi Memorial
Hall in February 1992. Both the friend and the father of his people,
Gandhi was a rare leader who chose to live in the midst of the masses,
sharing their sorrow and happiness and working to dispel the fear
of authority bred by long years of colonial rule. India's first prime
minister, Jawaharlal Nehru (1889–1964), considered Gandhi's

battle against fear his greatest gift to the Indian people. This may very well be true, since a strong, wise people undaunted by authority is essential in a democracy.

At a time like ours, growing access to unprecedented amounts of information makes it hard to deceive the people, who now have abundant opportunities to demonstrate their wisdom by advocating nonviolence.

GALTUNG: In October 1993, speaking as the first peace activist to address the Royal Military Academy of Spain, in Zaragoza, I proposed the following five elements for nonviolent intervention:

1. Some knowledge of military techniques is essential. Reducing violence necessitates knowledge of its technology.
2. It is vital to have knowledge of such police techniques as crowd control.
3. Knowledge of nonviolent approaches, such as Gandhi's *satyagraha*, is also important.
4. Another key point is having knowledge of conflict-resolution approaches, dispute settlement and so on.
5. Fifty per cent of the participants in such peacekeeping forces must be women.

The reaction from my Spanish audience was very positive. Gandhism and Buddhism inspire many, neither passive nor violent, middle ways. Today, unfortunately, primary attention is given to the first point. That is of course insufficient.

Philosophical Perspective

IKEDA: Displaying the kind of acumen to be expected from a person with his literary abilities and achievements, Vaclav Havel has said that the fountainhead of the violence that plagued socialist society was excessive reliance on theories and scientific knowledge. As he understands very well, knowledge of which we consider ourselves masters sometimes ends up mastering us. Too great a faith in theories can generate fanaticism and dogmatism that breed arrogant intolerance. But, in an essay that appeared in the Japanese journal *Sekai* (May 1992), Mr Havel has written to the effect that, now and probably always, life itself transcends the mere diagrams life-science produces and that science, which enabled humanity to unleash atomic energy, cannot prevent humanity from destroying itself with atomic weapons.

In *All Men Are Brothers* Gandhi said, 'Rationalists are admirable beings, rationalism is a hideous monster when it claims for itself omnipotence.' The same can be said of the theorist and short-sighted devotee of knowledge for its own sake. Because he realizes that knowledge, though important, must always be kept in philosophical perspective, Vaclav Havel can do much to help East Europe survive the labor-pangs of a newly emerging society.

GALTUNG: Life itself is the only absolute; and there is only one absolute perspective: the *dukkha–sukha* (suffering–happiness) dimension. Albert Schweitzer and Gandhi, as well as Buddhism, have all pointed this out and have argued for the negative option of suffering-reduction and the positive option of life-enhancement.

As you say, keeping things in philosophical perspective is important. Everything else is abstraction – capitalism, socialism, economic growth, classless society, state-run or private operation, and even human rights and democracy. None of these is absolute; all of them must be constantly reexamined in the light of the law of life.

Deifying abstractions and making absolute values of them is violence – cultural violence – and generates both direct and structural violence because it legitimizes either the one or the other. Occidental thought focuses on *ratio*, the reason. Male thinking focuses on axiomatic belief-systems. Consequently, as Carol Gilligan points out, we should be skeptical of occidental man, who is too willing to kill for such abstractions as democracy, human rights, capitalism, socialism and so on. Being an occidental male myself sometimes makes me very uneasy.

As to scientific knowledge, my position is a compromise. Let us assume that the only purpose of scientific pursuits – and of life itself – is the enhancement of life. Let us further assume that we have a hypothesis – perhaps human rights or democracy – for achieving this. I certainly would never declare that any hypothesis is true a priori and then treat it as a universal declaration for use in experimenting with the whole world.

If we compare peace to health and violence to disease, then medical science and peace science are similar enough to make a comparative example illuminating. Suppose a surgeon invents a new surgical procedure. I should be very disturbed if his or her scalpel programmed and controlled all scalpels everywhere so that, when this surgeon operated, the same operation was performed simultaneously all over the world.

This was the way Soviet politicians worked. Indeed, politicians in general constantly engage in a gigantic programme of experimentation on considerably weaker empirical and theoretical grounds than surgeons do. Perhaps modesty should keep experiments small. Perhaps the experimenters ought to have a sufficiently well-developed sense of responsibility to try their experiments on themselves first. Whenever politicians propose measures for certain social groups or nations, I always ask whether they are willing to try the same measures out on their own nations. If they are unwilling to take the medicine, why do they prescribe it for others? I am unwilling to abandon inductive-deductive thinking, though I recommend care and constant awareness of the possibility of error.

IKEDA: Throughout history, theories and knowledge, which are only symbols of parts of reality, have distorted human interpretations of the world as if they represented reality in its entirety. The tendency has been especially marked in Christianity. This is vividly evident in attempts to equate the part with the whole, as represented in the famous passage in the Gospel according to St John: 'and the Word was God'.

In contrast, oriental philosophy – especially Mahayana Buddhism – has been extremely cautious about trying to define verbally the force of life that essentially subsumes all theories and knowledge.

Existing since the time of Shakyamuni, this tendency reached a pinnacle in the thought of Nagarjuna (second or third century of the Common Era). In his penetrating search for reality, he exposed the fallacy of verbal expressions, which he sometimes went so far as to reject entirely. For instance, in a famous passage dealing with what is called the Middle Path of the Eightfold Negations, in the opening of his *Mula-madhyamaka-shastra*, he says that the Buddha transcends the fallacy of words to teach causal origination in the form of non-birth, non-extinction, non-cessation, non-permanence, non-uniformity, non-diversity, non-coming, and non-going.

Words always involve illusion. Realities fixed in verbal terms contain no certainties. Because its great teachers have realized this better than anyone else, Mahayana Buddhism is remote from the kinds of fanaticism and violence born of assigning absolute values to words and abstract concepts.

Reexamining everything in the light of the law of life, as you quite rightly insist, could make possible a revolution in our view of the world. We followers of Nichiren Daishonin's Buddhism believe in a law of life that is referred to in Japanese as *Myo-ho*, a term that includes the idea of a law of revival. Reexamining everything in the light of the Law of Life brings about a general revival of all things.

Of course, partial views of reality have values of their own and can undergo revival too when given their proper places within the overall law of life. Without evaluation in relation to that law, however, partial views masquerading as total concepts breed evil and unhappiness.

As a result of their searching examinations of limited views such as the idea that the 'Word is God', post-modernist Europeans are demonstrating increasing interest in Buddhism. This trend can contribute significantly to the world peace movement.

GALTUNG: Perhaps a deeper interest with Buddhism as one of its manifestations could make a similar significant contribution. Other manifestations of that deeper interest might be soft Christianity, like that of St Francis of Assisi or the Quakers – the Friends, as they are often called. Of course, growing interest in Buddhism is encouraging. But the nonviolent revolution that ended the Cold War was achieved by people who could hardly have read Gandhi. Something deeper inspired them. Part of their political culture had changed. As was not the case in Hungary, in 1956, both the peace movement and the dissident movement struggled nonviolently. Buddhism can change the world spiritual culture, but it is not alone in being able to do so. Let there be many voices and much dialogue!

Rights as Universal Norms

IKEDA: Karel Vasak, the French jurist, has developed a system according to which human rights are categorized in three generations. First-generation rights protect from coercion or oppression on the part of the national state. Such rights as freedom of religion, freedom of speech and so on fall into this category. Second-generation rights are related to fundamental aspects of existence and make demands on the national state: for instance, the elimination of social anomalies leading to such abuses as the exploitation of workers. Both categories involve negotiating with the state. Third-generation human rights, however, extend beyond the national framework. Operative on the global plane, they include the right to development, the right to a wholesome environment, the right to peace and the right to common ownership of the human heritage.

   In March 1992 the United Nations Commission on Human Rights issued a statement to the effect that human rights are universal, supernational norms and that, for this reason, their monitoring by international society is permissible even when this transgresses traditional taboos connected with respect for sovereignty or interference in internal affairs.

GALTUNG: Karel Vasak's scheme is very promising. But he is perhaps less than fully sensitive to certain other problems. One of these is the structure induced by the whole human-rights edifice. Another is the content of concrete norms. Both issues are characterized by the civilization that gave birth to the human-rights tradition: Greek origins, the French Enlightenment, the American and French constitutions, the Universal Declaration of 10 December 1948 and the Human Rights Covenants of 16 December 1966. All of these correspond to Vasak's first and second generations.

The whole construction is an ingenious way of linking international and national law. The United Nations General Assembly, as supreme lawmaker, invites states to ratify human-rights instruments in return for recognition of their good standing in the world body. National states are bound to extend rights to their citizens, who are entitled to bring court cases against governments that fail to implement human-rights provisions. In principle, therefore, human-rights accords establish not only a social contract between governments and their citizens, but also an international contract between those governments and the United Nations. In short, two birds with one stone, apologizing for the violent expression.

The reverse of this brilliant coin bears less attractive aspects. One is the verticality of the construction. Instead of chains and cycles of mutual rights and obligations based perhaps on empathy or compassion, these accords are judiciable, legal rules to be guarded by all kinds of governmental and nongovernmental organizations. The construction reinforces the division of the world into states by making them accountable in both directions – upward to the United Nations and downward to their own citizens – and by making them, if not the providers, at least the guarantors of human-rights implementation.

Missing from this entire picture are compassion, direct concern and care of everyone by everyone – elements much closer to Buddhist and feminist ideas. Because of their absence, I entertain nightmare visions of armies of lawyers litigating for citizens squabbling over rights. Nonetheless, there can be no doubt that we require human-rights accords as one form of protection.

Another less pleasing aspect of the structure is the demands imposed by states on 'their' citizens in return for generously extended human rights. Among these demands are taxes; compulsory military service (which emerged as early as 1793 in France) for any and all purposes the government decides to identify with 'national interests'; and of course general respect for the state that has 'generously' given the citizens their rights.

One of the most disturbing facets of the construction as it exists today is the areas in which it lacks content. For instance, it makes no provisions for the rights of nonhuman life. It has been very slow to make specific statements about the rights of women and children and remains silent on the rights of indigenous peoples.

Above all, human rights as stated are individualist and pay insufficient attention to the collective rights of groups. They concentrate on general privileges available to the Westerner but not provided to others. How the right to education can be implemented is a useful example. In Norway, members of the minority people called the Sami (Lapps is a derogatory expression sometimes used by non-Sami peoples) have the right to attend Norwegian schools where they are taught, in Norwegian, how to live a Norwegian lifestyle. This is one interpretation of the right to education. It is quite another matter, however, to ensure that the Sami as a group have their own schools where they learn in Sami languages (as distinct from merely being taught Sami) how to lead a Sami way of life.

The many other kinds of rights missing from the contemporary construction – the right of the elderly to live out their lives with their families, the right of children to homes free from divorce, and so on – make the Western nations look less perfect than they like to think they are. As set forth now, statements of human rights appear to be disciplining, controlling, Westernizing instruments that, far from being universal, bear the unmistakable stamp of the people who compiled them; that is, middle-aged Western males, now mainly dead, with university educations anchored in a given period of Western history.

For this reason, I am skeptical about using such statements of rights as international instruments to adjudicate on, sentence and punish nations. I have no objection to resolutions, admonitions and dialogues. But the violent enforcement of peace and imposition of human rights are problematic, to say the least. Indeed, the very terms themselves are oxymoronic. Attempts to carry out such processes become all the more dubious when one group of countries – most of them former colonial powers – castigates another group of countries – many of them former colonies.

Given such circumstances, developing nations soon learn how to castigate in their turn and will speedily begin looking for places to practice what they have learned. The Iraqis learned from British colonialists the use of gas to put down popular revolts. Still later, after having been exposed to a Western military machine with United Nations Security Council legitimation, Saddam Hussein immediately used the techniques he had learned from the British against the Kurds and Shi'ites. Having said this, however, I realize the need for the international community to come to the rescue of people such as those Kurds and Shi'ites, or the Jews under the Nazi regime.

IKEDA: In spite of the objections you raise about the shortcomings of the codex of human rights the West has compiled, I am convinced the time has come for us to revise the view that guaranteeing human rights is a purely domestic national issue. Human rights must be regarded as international and global. As if to symbolize this need, 1993 was designated International Year of Aboriginal Peoples; and a World Human Rights Conference was held in Vienna that

June. All over a world beset with regional and ethnic conflicts, the cry has gone forth for moral intervention when minorities are oppressed or human rights are infringed.

In an article on the Yugoslavian conflict in the *International Herald Tribune* in December 1992, my good friend Professor Joseph Nye, of Harvard, said that their complexity compels us to reinterpret the old liberal reliance on the right to racial self-determination as the solution to ethnic issues. He proposes that we replace this approach with international guarantees of human rights and minority rights. I think he has a very good point.

Of course, solutions are hard to find for multi-ethnic conflicts. Nonetheless, all the combatants in the former Yugoslavia once lived together peacefully. And if they pool their wisdom, I feel certain they can work out a system for doing so again.

The League of Nations had an organization for ensuring minority rights. Perhaps it would be a good idea to establish a United Nations High Commission for Minorities and Aboriginal Peoples to work cooperatively with the High Commission for Refugees to provide international guarantees for the rights of these groups.

GALTUNG: Trouble arises when human rights are forcibly imposed. The nations of the former Yugoslavia need compassion more than military intervention. Ever since the schism between Catholic and Orthodox Christianity in 1054, and the Crusades against Islam, starting in 1095, their karma has been horrible. Generally they have not lived in peace at all, except when forced to do so by the Ottomans, the Habsburgs or Marshal Tito (1892–1980).

Divisions imposed from without by events occurring nine centuries ago continue to fracture former Yugoslavia in general and Bosnia-Herzegovina in particular. The condition of the people there calls for more understanding and less moral condemnation. Economic sanctions will only unify them and strengthen their resolve – in addition to killing, slowly, the aged, the weak and the sick.

Japanese Views of Human Rights

IKEDA: In the name of development, industrialized nations pour vast amounts of aid money into developing nations. As a consequence, compelled to struggle with ever-burgeoning debts, developing nations see their peoples grow poorer as multinational business corporations derive all their profits from aid-financed development projects. Far from attempting to correct pollution and damage to traditional lifestyles caused by such projects, some Third World governments side with developers and discourage conservationists in all possible ways. The poorest and weakest levels of society pay the environmental price. Realizing its frequently vicious effects, some people are calling for a halt to official developmental aid.

Since Japan is both a notorious consumer of natural resources and the largest provider of developmental aid in the world, Japanese attitudes toward human rights, at home and abroad, are being closely scrutinized. The people of Japan have never struggled to wrest their rights from their rulers. Indeed, they were nearly two centuries later than the French in receiving constitutional guarantees of basic human rights. Even when finally granted, such legal assurances were the result of external, not internal, pressure. They were therefore externally, not internally generated.

I do not entirely agree with Western revisionists who insist that Japan and the Japanese are too culturally different from the rest of the world to deal with successfully. I suspect Western advocates of this approach of trying to thrust their own ways of thinking down other peoples' throats. Perhaps they have forgotten the evils of old-fashioned imperialism and colonialism. Instead of accepting the 'hopeless difference' theory, it is more accurate to stress a certain time-lag in Japanese awareness of human rights.

Be that as it may, our partners in Asia and Africa, as well as in the industrialized West, doubt the impartiality of Japanese recognition of universal human rights. Max V. Soliven, publisher and editorial chairman of the *Philippine Star*, gives a good idea of the unfortunately fairly widespread distrust in the following passage, taken from *Japan and the World in the Post-Cold War Era*:

> These days, gleaming jet aircraft unload battalions of blue-suited businessmen from Edo [Tokyo] and the bustling industrial complexes of the Kansai plain, as well as Kagoshima in the far south, who may look like civilians but possess the decided swagger of the old *kempeitai* [military police].

As long as we are seen in this light, we Japanese will find it hard to shed our reputation for human-rights backwardness and insensitivity to the sufferings of others.

GALTUNG: Let me first say that development is closely, but mainly positively, related to the implementation of human rights. I cannot cite a single case from economic history in which anything that can be called true development has resulted from foreign-aid donors' making all local decisions and even competing with each other to convert local economies into export economies geared toward the earning of 'badly needed hard currency'. I am one of those people calling for an end to official developmental aid, except as compassionate emergency assistance in time of catastrophe.

Often aid sets up a vicious circle in which economic assistance has such disastrous environmental consequences as to necessitate still further developmental aid. Third World elites who stand to benefit directly from such projects are at least as guilty as the aid donors in these crimes against people and nature.

It is necessary to take a critical view of the human-rights tradition. Japan has always been highly vertically structured socially, with the emperor or shogun and his retinue at the top. During the Edo period (1615–1867), the top echelon was supported by a vertical social structure, beginning with the samurai class and descending through the peasant, artisan and merchant classes to end in a group of outcasts (including various *gaijin* or foreigners) at the bottom. A true social contract between the emperor and the citizens might have saved Japan and Japan's victims from the Pacific War of 1931–45.

This might have been so, but doubt persists. Even had Japan been equipped with human-rights machinery, the general population might still have agreed with the militarist expansionist policy. The only difference might have been better treatment of dissidents. Like the rest of the West, the United States lays great stress on human rights, yet intervenes militarily in the affairs of other nations about once a year.

It may be that Mr Soliven of the *Philippine Star* confuses an economic with a military invasion. There is a difference. Today the Japanese carry in their luggage not the swaggering bravado of the *kempeitai*, but a technically very superior economy able to compete, in an astounding variety of products, with all other economies in the world. After all, the Japanese have reduced the trade pattern of the once economically mighty United States to that of a rich Third World country which must even beg to export rice and logs, and bully Japan to import cellular telephones.

The Japanese businessmen Mr Soliven mentions and their political leaders certainly believe in world trade and competition, but are ideologically blinded to certain negative side-effects of their actions: not only conflicts with the United States and other Organization for Economic Cooperation and Development (OECD) countries, but also their impact on Third World countries. In the Philippines, for instance, the Japanese remove – often with the co-operation of local elites – agricultural and marine resources badly needed by the Philippine people themselves. Mr Soliven overlooks a point in the passage you quote: lack of compassion for the poor.

Nonetheless, the insensitivity of Japanese and other business people to the impact of their economic activities cannot be excused. The Japanese are good at eclecticism. They skillfully combine both a market and a planned economy. Perhaps they would benefit from combining capitalistic philosophy with a little Marxist insight into the way capitalism works deep down in society, particularly in the societies on the periphery of Japan. Although many people believe they do, Marxism and capitalism do not exclude each other. Wedded to Buddhist insights, the two would make a great deal of good sense together.

IKEDA: You know the Japanese and Japan, and your observations are fair and accurate. Still, I am afraid what you say will please only the Japanese who dismiss all foreign criticism of our human-rights philosophy and our backwardness in this field as just more Japan-bashing.

In his *Bunmei-ron no Gairaku* (Summarized Cultural theory), the enlightened Japanese philosopher and educator Yukichi Fukuzawa (1835–1901) divided civilization into the external and the internal. In the former category he included everything from clothing, food and drink, machinery and housing to government ordinances and laws; that is, all those things that can be seen and heard. In the second category, he put the temperament and the general knowledge and virtue of a people. He said, 'Whereas exterior civilization is easy to obtain, inner civilization is difficult to come by.' He further insisted, with regard to their attempt to modernize at the end of the nineteenth century (the process called *bunmei kaika*, or civilization and enlightenment), that the Japanese should accomplish the difficult first and postpone the easy.

Examining Japan today, we observe that the nation has done an excellent job of exterior modernization but that problems remain in connection with acquiring the right 'temperament'. Fukuzawa bemoaned the feudal servility that made people 'stand when ordered to stand and dance when told to dance just as servilely as a scrawny domesticated dog'. How far we have progressed from that servility is open to debate.

Institutionally, Japan is now a democracy in which fundamental human rights are constitutionally protected. As I have already implied, the problem is that the institutions and the constitution have not come about from within as a result of an elevation of the general knowledge and virtue of the people. After defeat in World War II, the occupation forces provided a windfall in the form of a constitution. The people of Japan did not earn it with their own sweat and blood.

The words and deeds of Japanese abroad – especially politicians – cast doubt on their understanding of human rights. The same lack of understanding is behind many of the faults of our society, symbolized perhaps by bullying in schools and by salaried men who actually overwork themselves to death (so-called *karo-shi*).

Chomin Nakae (1847–1901), a champion of liberal popular rights, described the concept of human rights in Japan in the following way: 'Human rights may be "endowed" from above or they may be "retrieved" through struggle. The former are inferior to the latter. But, if repeated effort is exerted to maintain "endowed" rights, they may rank with "retrieved" rights.'

The philosophy of human rights cannot be said to have taken deep root in the minds of the Japanese people. Converting 'endowed' rights into 'retrieved' rights is a psychological task the Japanese have been facing since the middle of the nineteenth century and the initiation of the modernization program.

GALTUNG: If I were Japanese, I might stress this point, too. As a Westerner, however, I perceive the self-righteous Japan-bashing attitude of the West only too clearly. As a citizen of the world, I would join you in seeing two truths – one critical of Japan, the other critical of the West – that are not mutually exclusive.

Philosophical Basis

IKEDA: The declaration on development and rights adopted by the General Assembly of the United Nations in 1986 clearly states that the individual human being – and not the national state or any other group – is the central subject of the right to development.

You have said that development must mean the development of human nature and that such social processes as production and distribution are only means for the improvement of humanity. In addition, you have said that the foundation of human rights ought to be the preservation of opportunities for self-realization. Provision of such opportunities under just and equitable circumstances is a prime value of peace.

But social-structural changes without a sound philosophical basis produce only limited results. The Buddhist spirit of compassion means empathizing totally with the sufferings of others and being willing to do everything possible to alleviate such suffering. This strikes me as an excellent basis for a philosophy oriented toward ensuring universal human rights.

GALTUNG: Generally speaking, there are three ways of justifying human rights.

First, they may be justified on the basis of authority; that is, human rights are correct because the United Nations General Assembly has agreed on them and/or they derive from the American and French revolutionary traditions. I do not find this intellectually or morally satisfactory because – among other reasons – it justifies Western biases. All the authorities on which such justification is based are dead Western males; like, for example, the French statesman René

Cassin (1887–1976), key author of the Universal Declaration of Human Rights issued by the United Nations on 10 December 1948.

Second, human rights may be deduced from first principles – innate freedom and equality or rationality of human beings, and so on. The problem with this approach is, once again, the need to justify the first principles. The ones I have mentioned bear the imprint of a certain period of Western history, the Enlightenment, and are therefore problematic if human rights are to be considered universal.

Third, we may attempt to justify them on the basis of functional relations to the needs of human and nonhuman nature; in other words, the law of life. This is the approach I try in my *Human Rights in Another Key*. Two basic problems arise in connection with it: identifying more or less universal human needs; and empirically demonstrating that implementation of human rights serves those needs. The foundation of this method of justification is less shaky than those of the other two. The first two approaches may lead to the illusion that human rights are eternally the same everywhere. The third, however, is so fraught with problems that its catalogue of human rights must be constantly revised. I find that good. As Albert Einstein pointed out, ethical principles must be tested empirically and revised according to the outcomes of the examinations.

Let us look at some examples of where this approach leads. If we begin with the need to survive, we immediately see that peace is a primary requirement for the human condition itself. Examining well-being and its components, we begin to see a social construction in which priority must be given to production for the satisfaction of basic needs. No piece of land should be entrusted to producers of coffee beans or to speculators until we are certain that the basic needs – say for edible beans – have been met. Priority must be given to a clean environment where essential air and water are neither scarce nor polluted. Rights of this kind deal with material-somatic needs.

Then there are the human spirit's needs for identity and freedom. Just as I do not accept the Maslowian assumption of hierarchy, where mental needs are ranked above those of the body, so I do not assign lower priorities to spiritual needs. What demands does the insurance of those rights impose on the social construction? I think smaller, more tightly woven social units are most conducive to their insurance.

In a sense, I reverse Karel Vasak's generations. Beginning with the need for peace – his third generation – I move on to development and the environment – the second generation – to guarantee just distribution of goods. With what I call nonmaterial needs, we have arrived at Vasak's first generation, which is focused on the right to identify and to unify with whatever the individual chooses. This is tantamount to a somewhat broad formulation of the freedom of faith. Then we arrive at very basic freedoms: the right to move and the freedom to be impressed by phenomena and to express our feelings about them. These are important, hard-won rights that must never be given up.

The gist of my critique of human rights is not to take away any rights already achieved, but to add to the list of rights and to give much higher priority to Vasak's third generation. In addition, I believe in universality, but only after dialogues have been conducted and the values of other civilizations have come to be understood and – to some extent – accepted as contributions as important as those from the West.

So far, I have mentioned only human needs. But nonhuman nature, too, has basic needs of its own. I am not speaking of nature as a servant or slave to be treated well only in order to allow human beings to grow and develop in a 'sustainable manner'. If we are interested in nature for its own sake, we find ourselves confronting the problem of enhancing the environment – as we cynically call it – by taking from nature only those things that nature freely gives. This is the Buddhist norm.

Human beings are more powerful than other species. But our power ought to inspire in us a sense of responsibility instead of breeding arrogance and corruption. So far, we have mainly enslaved nature. For example, in our struggle against epidemic diseases, though it was a close call during the plague years in the Europe of the 1340s, instead of being done in by it, we gradually attacked the causes and finally eliminated the disease.

Buddhism comes closer than any other philosophy to a comprehensive human-rights philosophy. But only Westerners who are capable of breaking out of the mental traps of their tradition find this philosophy accessible. Because it crosses all seven fault-lines in the human construction by being inter-species, inter-gender, inter-generation, inter-class, inter-race, inter-national and inter-country, Buddhism offers great potential for a universal rights concept. Since it focuses on the Chain of Life, Buddhism is obviously inter-generational. Women are the queen-pins of this Chain and, like the Chain itself, are fundamental to Buddhism. (Buddhist scriptures, like all others written mainly by men, are not explicit on this point.) Imbued with the spirit of compassion (*karuna*), Buddhism's whole social philosophy bridges all the other fault-lines.

IKEDA: While appreciating your evaluation and respecting your views that the presently accepted concept of human rights has served to justify Western prejudices and bears the imprint of certain phases of Western history, I nonetheless believe firmly in the universal value of human rights. Certainly Western civilization has been guilty of great crimes against indigenous peoples and has a

grave responsibility to bear in connection with such horrors as the
slave trade and the subjugation of local populations – the Incas,
for example. Still, as Arthur M. Schlesinger, Jr. has said, the West
has produced its own antidotes. One of the finest of these is the
Universal Declaration of Human Rights, which states in its first
article that all human beings are born free and are equal in rights
and dignity. It can be inferred from this statement that the declaration clearly rejects discrimination against women, children,
refugees, the handicapped, foreigners and so on.

   To eliminate violations and restore their dignity, rights must be
just. The same first article of the Universal Declaration urges all
people to act together in a spirit of mutual fellowship under the
guidance of reason and conscience.

   As is widely recognized and often commented on, rights inevitably
entail duties. In discussing the rights guaranteed to the citizens,
the Japanese constitution points out the duty to use those rights
always for the public welfare. I consider this injunction wise, since
we require not only the strength to stand up for our just rights, but
also the internal standards of justice to examine the ends to which
we exercise those rights.

   Simone Weil (1909–43), French philosopher and mystic, has said
that the idea of duties takes precedence over the idea of rights and
that humanism divorced from religion is evil. The American poet
Walt Whitman (1819–92) said its religious element is the ultimate
essence of democracy and called for the revival of a deeper, more
generous and nobler faith generated by a new power. This linking
of rights, duties and religion reinforces my conviction that humanism
and democracy can be realized only with the aid of a living religious
faith that cultivates internal standards.

   In my novel *The Human Revolution*, I express my belief in the
efficacy of Nichiren Daishonin's Buddhism in this context:

> The Buddhism of Nichiren Daishonin is by no means a religion
> for the sake of religion or for the sake of power or authority. It
> is not a religion for the sake of any specific race or nation. It is
> a religion for the sake of humanity, the human race, and human
> rights.

   The well-spring of all Soka Gakkai International activity is the
spirit of Nichiren Daishonin and of the Lotus Sutra manifested in
the will to lead all peoples to happiness. I believe this to be the essence
of the kind of true humanism necessary for the creation of an age
dedicated to universal human rights.

GALTUNG: Your concept of universal human rights is deeper and
broader than the one set forth in the Universal Declaration of
Human Rights of 1948. I agree with you and believe that the time

has come for Buddhism to participate fully in the debate on rights. I look forward to still more comprehensive universal declarations. The process of setting forth and recognizing human rights is continuous. There can never be a final document. But there can be better dialogue as part of a process toward better declarations.

CHAPTER 6

A New World Order

After Socialism

IKEDA: Some Russians call the collapse of the Soviet Union the ultimate termination of the French Revolution. There is a modicum of appropriateness in the idea. The end of the USSR completely discredited the once dominant notion that the proletariat Russian Revolution was an extension and further development of the bourgeois French Revolution.

Whether market principles or liberal democratic ideas can serve as the foundation of a new world order remains uncertain. Erupting nationalist energies are far more destructive than constructive. And the outlook is one of continued groping in the dark in East Europe during the last years of the twentieth century.

In his widely discussed essay 'The End of History?', Francis Fukuyama, then employed on the planning staff of the United States Department of State, expresses the opinion that the Soviet Union's divesting itself of socialism in favor of Western-style liberal democracy signifies the end of progress and development of the principles and systems that constitute the basis of history. According to Fukuyama, history interpreted as a progressive process has reached its final conclusion. I find this a biased view.

GALTUNG: In spite of his Japanese name, Fukuyama is an archetypical occidental thinker. He believes that all historical processes ultimately reach a final stage (*Endzustand*, as the Germans say), with one form triumphant. He is a Hegelian. But it must be remembered that, like Marx, Georg Hegel (1770–1831) had a very incomplete version of dialectics. According to Hegel, only one aspect of the world is dialectic, as reflected in the four stages of world history dear to both philosophers. Furthermore, he insisted that the dialectic suddenly stops at an *Endzustand*.

This very idea contrasts sharply with the Daoist interpretation according to which everything is yin–yang – including yin and yang themselves. The yin–yang series goes on and on without a final stage: one becomes two, then becomes one again before becoming two again, and so on. When harmony is established by the bridging of one yin–yang fault-line, another fault-line will either open or be

114

reactivated. I find this a very realistic image of social reality. The dialectic operative in this system never stops. Our task is to steer it nonviolently toward higher levels.

Fukuyama's is a very Western theory indeed. And as might be expected, the final stage where history ends just happens to be a triumphant liberal, democratic, market system, like that of the United States.

Hegel, his mentor, thought the final system would be something like the Prussian state. Interestingly, though he spoke much about people in higher and lower positions (*Herr und Knecht*), Hegel never discovered the phenomenon of exploitation. This was for Marx to uncover and to incorporate in his dialectic of historical materialism. Hegel's final stage entails a council of wise men running the world, not unlike the State Department planning staff where Fukuyama was the number-two man. What emerges in Fukuyama's highly forgettable – and already, practically speaking, forgotten – work is an image of the world as the United States writ large. And this is precisely what one might expect from a person with the author's background.

It behooves us to take a more realistic view of history than the Hegelian one espoused by Francis Fukuyama. Examine, for instance, medieval, feudal European society with its estates: clergy, aristocracy, burghers; to which could be added common working people – and presumably a fifth group made up of women, children and such outsiders as Moors, Jews and Gypsies. Still further down the scale, as always in the Christian world, came the nonhuman environment of animals, plants, forests, water, air and outer space.

For ages, the estates were figuratively aboil. The process took centuries, but finally the aristocrats shouldered the clergy aside. In the eighteenth century, burghers residing behind city walls pulled the aristocrats down to the level of mere *hommes* or *citoyens*, numerically too few to dominate a head-counting democracy. In the nineteenth century, armed with the ideas of communism, socialism and social democracy, and with such tools as trade unions, the working people struggled to become good bourgeois. And in our own century the struggle goes on, as minority groups of all kinds, women and children strive to make themselves heard. Viewed in this broad perspective, therefore, the Russian Revolution of 1917 can be regarded as the sequel of the French Revolution of 1789.

This more realistic view of European history reveals five levels where four processes take place but by no means result in a termination of the historical process itself. Socially sidetracked, aristocrats and the clergy became arrogant, intellectual professionals. The aristocrats became equally arrogant bureaucrats, and the burghers of yesterday are today's corporate capitalists. The boiling down process inevitably begins again, though it probably will not follow past precedents.

With the support of some intellectuals, the military branch of the bureaucracy clings to fundamental faith in its entitlement to send young men anywhere to kill combatants and noncombatants with ever more sophisticated killing machines. Governments believe that the human rights they extend to their peoples entitle them to demand and receive general obedience to their military exploits. The globalization of the military in coalitions such as the ones formed for the Gulf War in 1991 and for operations in Somalia in 1992, legitimized by the United Nations Security Council, does not change reality. Killing is still killing. Moreover, there is no cause to worry about the end of history. History moves on, as any one piece splits horizontally or vertically into two, and struggle, unification and division repeat themselves. The only alteration is an increase in scale. A globalized economy does not eliminate class, it globalizes it. At least it does this for the upper classes, and one day perhaps even the proletariat may be globalized.

East Europe lagged behind in the historical processes outlined above. After the grip of feudalism was relaxed, the East followed the course pursued earlier by the West, but with variations. For example, its capitalism was headed not by a monarch, such as a Queen Elizabeth I, but by a secretary-general. This social phase was referred to not as early state-capitalism, but as socialism. Whereas in Western Europe state-capitalism had preceded, in Eastern Europe it followed early private capitalism, thus paving the way for the next phase of capitalism, the one being experienced there now.

At present, Eastern Europe is undergoing transition from a brutally commanded socialism directed from the top of society to an equally brutally commanded capitalism directed from the tops of some societies in the West. National struggles are in part linked to this phenomenon, since the element of class always persists and since human beings tend to blame their frustrations on someone else.

Eastern Europe is now working its way into periphery capitalism, out of which it will probably have to work itself some day, as the Third World has been trying to do and as much of East Asia has successfully done. We cannot know the nature of the East's post-capitalism phase. Given our present knowledge of the horrors capitalism has perpetrated since the time of Columbus on human beings, nations and the natural environment in peripheral regions, we should long ago have begun trying to enter a new phase. Instead of doing so, however, though no less a failure than socialism, capitalism has more cleverly exported its problems to the periphery, which has been and remains often too weak to cope with the situation.

IKEDA: Taking the broad yin–yang view of history has meaning of its own, but this cannot justify merely looking idly on during such processes as you mention: when one becomes two, two becomes one and so on. It behooves all of us to do what we can to direct the development of history in promising directions.

In the 1960s the formerly apparently monolithic communist Chinese philosophy was split into two rival factions, one headed by Mao Zedong and the other by Liu Xiaoqi. This spirit unleashed the tempest of the Cultural Revolution, which in some respects resembled the Stalinist purges of the 1930s. Conflicting reports make it impossible to judge accurately the numbers of victims of this tragic course of action. The experience is still too vivid to permit generalization, but surely only the most prejudiced and desperate can pretend that the Red Guard did more good than harm. We must never forget the hellish suffering that can lurk behind the seemingly simple process of splitting one into two.

Only pretenders to godlike omniscience claim to be able to foresee history's direction. Marxists, confident of the correctness of their views, predicted that history would logically follow the path of materialistic dialectic development. They were mistaken. And it may be just as mistaken to equate the downfall of socialism with the triumph of liberalism and the end of history.

In spite of the difficulty of foreseeing future events, however, we must try to orient the course of history. If we do not, we may miss precious opportunities to improve the human condition and, as a lateral consequence, rob the study of history of all meaning.

GALTUNG: I certainly agree. But there was more to the Cultural Revolution than rival factions. A class of intellectual bureaucrats – the mandarins – ruled China for 2,000–3,000 years. Instead of changing this, Mao's 1949 revolution introduced 'red mandarins'. Rural youth revolted against this, and between 1966 and 1969 brought about the terrible consequences you describe. But the problem of rule by a class of bureaucratic intellectuals persists, and one day China will have to find a solution to it.

IKEDA: Yes, the German sociologist Eduard Heimann has significant comments to make on this issue in his book *Soziale Theorie der Wirtschaftssysteme*. He identifies modern Europe-dominated civilization as a highly distinctive 'economistic' system distinct from integrational systems found in other societies. The sole driving principle behind the Western economist system is expansion pursued for its own sake in what Heimann calls a purposeless, blind and ruinous dynamic. While making possible the material prosperity enjoyed by some peoples in the world today, the system has upset the overall balance of human life by stimulating excessive devel-

opment of its economic aspects. Sooner or later, this discrimina-
tive system will be compelled to shift in the direction of an integrative
social system under a new guise.

Heimann has a point. Still, we must neither underestimate nor
ignore such merits of the modern economistic system as reductions
in sickness and hunger in many parts of the world. When it arrives,
the new integrative system must not turn its back on the good its
predecessor has accomplished. Instead, it must evolve dialecti-
cally from a foundation composed of the merits of the economistic
system. Although there is an element of over-optimism in it, from
the standpoint of a person who hopes that the twenty-first century
will be characterized by intensified care for the needs of life in all
its manifestations, I agree in general with Heimann's evaluation of
the modern age.

GALTUNG: So do I, though I should like to make a comment.
Deeply rooted in Western civilization, expansionism actually
predates the evolution of our current economism. For instance, it
is at least as old as the missionary command in Matthew XXVIII:19:
'Go ye therefore, and make disciples of the nations.' Unreflecting
acceptance of expansion and growth for its own sake frightens me.
Furthermore, I am afraid that health benefits come in spite of, and
not because of, economism. Both the positive and the negative
aspects of the situation are real. Our task is to steer the dialectic
toward greater life-enhancement for all.

The Rights of the Whole Human Race

IKEDA: Confronted with frustration and obstructions at home,
Mikhail S. Gorbachev achieved great things in the field of international diplomacy. Most brilliant of his achievements was his
courageous shift of emphasis from the interests of limited national
and political groups to those of all humanity. He realized that no
amount of assiduous work in the name of the class struggle and
the international communist movement can protect humanity from
nuclear destruction. The very magnitude of that threat might make
the path Gorbachev chose seem all too obvious, but no one else
had dared embark upon it. Gorbachev deserves immense credit for
originating a bold new diplomacy that roused his country from its
ideologically hidebound condition and helped his people and the
rest of the world to see the obvious at last.

Gorbachev's diplomacy led to the sudden collapse of the Berlin
Wall, the domino-like downfall of East European communist
regimes and the end of the Cold War. Before these developments,
the United Nations had often been little more than a sparring

ground for the Soviet and American blocs. Today, however, the role of the revitalized United Nations takes on greater significance with each passing day.

The expansion of the United Nation's role in world affairs symbolizes the pressing need to give precedence in all considerations to the interests of the entire human race. This is especially true in connection with environmental problems, which, in the opinions of some, pose a graver threat than nuclear warfare.

We must remember that, as was proclaimed by a group of non-governmental organizations at a preparatory conference for the Rio de Janeiro World Summit, 'The problems of the environment are the problems of humanity.' In reorienting emphasis toward the interests of all humankind, Gorbachev's leadership is very encouraging to those of us who would like to promote de-emphasis of the sovereign national or ethnic state for the sake of greater emphasis on the welfare of the human race in general.

GALTUNG: Certainly the way Gorbachev reoriented the international discourse was amazing. Perhaps he was the only statesman in the world capable of seeing the interests of the whole human race, beyond national and class distinctions. The speech he delivered before the United Nations in 1988 is one of the greatest documents of our times. Regrettably, while he was speaking, the then US president and vice-president, Ronald Reagan and George Bush, were not listening – as they certainly should have been – but were discussing a photo opportunity in front of the Statue of Liberty.

Thinking, talking and acting in the interests of the whole human race are good; but results often depend very much on who is thinking, talking and acting. For instance, the task of the United Nations should never be killing in 'enforcement actions', but ought to be promoting peace through peaceful means. This is why I do not consider it to have been the Security Council's work to legitimate massive killing in Resolution 678, concerning the war in the Persian Gulf. Saddam Hussein was exceptionally brutal, but I understand he was willing to negotiate on at least four, separate, good opportunities. Nonetheless, the allied coalition in general and the United States in particular were unwilling to negotiate because they were out to punish, in the name of the human race, a client who had gone sour.

In connection with class distinctions, I can only say that the class struggle itself persists even when it disappears from public discourse. In the very same fashion, patriarchy existed long before people like Ibsen started talking about it. Until solutions are found, class will remain a recurring social reality because, among other reasons, some people have more and some less, and some people have more precisely because others have less. One formula that works in some countries and is good as long as it is not detrimental to nature and the Third World is a combination of social capitalism to produce wealth and social democracy to distribute it. Add ecological awareness to this formula, and the result can be a fairly decent society.

Fires of Nationalism

IKEDA: The end of the Cold War has removed the danger of a holocaust in the name of ideologies only to replace it with the perils of rampant nationalism released by the removal of ideological restraints. As an example of the energy of Arab nationalism, the terrifying Gulf War made us all aware of the complex difficulties involved in building a new post-Cold War world order.

Diverse and widespread independence uprisings sparked by the collapse of the Soviet Union symbolize the shift from an age of ideologies to an age of nationalist problems. National identity is deep-rooted. But, as Iraq's Saddam Hussein makes painfully clear, narrow, dogmatic nationalism poses a threat to peace in general.

The tumult of the past few years has proved the former French president, Charles de Gaulle, correct in having described ethnic affiliations as far stronger than ideologies. Nationalism is powerful and can be ominous. But I am convinced education can deal with it effectively. Culture, the foundation of nationalism, is largely acquired. And education can alter or mold acquired traits. Different ethnic groups need not always relate to each other as dominators and dominated. History offers many instances in which, though perhaps imperfectly, different peoples have worked out systems for harmonious coexistence. Overcoming the dilemma of nationalism confronting the new world order is an issue of maximum importance.

GALTUNG: An ideology can best be understood in terms of what it omits. For instance, liberalism is reticent on exploitation and Marxism on freedom. One is silent on areas on which the other is eloquent, and both are very reticent on the inner human being.

A typical ideology, nationalism interprets the world in terms of the culturally and ethnically defined self and other, viewed as good and bad respectively. It is as eloquently silent on the bad aspects of the self as it is on the good aspects of the other. Science may provide one way to remove blinkers of this kind. If so, scientists, or any others who attempt that task, must not expect to become popular, especially when they illuminate unflattering aspects of the self-images of their own people and the ideologies of their own elites.

The Cold War – or Frozen Peace, as I prefer to call it – kept local nationalism at a low temperature by outlawing it in the name of loyalties to alliances. The socialist illusion was to believe that class is the only fault-line that matters. When the Cold War ended, the East, which had been more repressive and where there are more different nationalities, witnessed the greater explosion. But other nationalities are articulating themselves forcefully outside East Europe, too – for example the Scots, Irish, Bretons, Corsicans, Catalans and Basques. Indeed, until recently it was not the Balkans but Ulster, where the Catholic–Protestant fault-line is sharpest, even hot, that was the hottest spot of unrest in Europe.

Societies that presumed and declared nationalism to be unimportant promoted the idea of the classless society. Today societies presuming class to be unimportant promote the idea of national separatism. Both will be equally disappointed because both class and nationalism matter, as do gender, generation, relation to nature, race and territory. All these factors exist in the shadows of history. They are in its waiting room, waiting to be heard from.

Whether it is class or nationalism that receives greater emphasis depends on various factors. Recent neglect of one of these aspects tends to intensify the importance of one or the other when it finally arrives in the spotlight. Long-sustained attention reduces the imperative nature of either, especially if extended deliberation seems to indicate either that a solution is imminent or that no solution at all is possible. For instance, the Nordic countries fought with and dominated each other for centuries before finally achieving a kind of confederation – the Nordic Council – making active co-existence possible. Today these divides are pacified. But we cannot expect this condition to persist forever, especially if the divides are ignored and peace is taken for granted.

Whether nationalism or class is more important depends on who you are. It is scarcely surprising that Charles de Gaulle, a representative of the upper classes in an intensely nationalist country, cared little about class: he had all he needed. But he was an avid nationalist.

As you say, Arab nationalism certainly exists and may some day result in an Arab Union. The European Union transcending the nation state also exists now that the Maastricht Treaty on an ever closer union has been ratified. The union I speak of is based on European supernationalism; that is, the nationalism of the European superstate. By the end of the twentieth century, it will be fully equipped with its own, probably nuclear-armed, military. True, the European Union makes war between France and Germany highly unlikely; but it does not eliminate the possibility of a war conducted jointly by France and Germany. A nascent Franco-German army will probably be the nucleus of the future European army. Belgium and Luxembourg, Spain and Italy are joining. European nationalist arrogance is surfacing in such writings as Jacques Duroselle's *L'Europe: Histoire de ses peuples*, which deprecates the horrors of the

Inquisition, witch-hunts, colonialism and slavery, and attempts to interpret European history as a long march toward the ultimate goal of the European Union. The best way to approach the European Union is either to stay out of it or to vote against it, as the Danes did in June 1992. The world does not need more superpowers. It needs smaller, diverse units that are linked symbiotically and equitably.

IKEDA: In contrast to people who remain eloquently silent on their own demerits and the merits of others, Gandhi took a diminishing view – as if through the wrong end of a telescope – of the faults of others, while examining his own with a magnifying lens. This is another instance of his tough but modest sense of honor at work.

Of course, fanatics behave in a diametrically opposed fashion. They magnify and exaggerate others' failings – sometimes to the extent of invention – while minimizing and even entirely overlooking the most fatal of their own faults. Education is the only key to the prevention of such abuses. I mean not merely schooling but education in the broad sense as understood by such teachers of humanity as Shakyamuni and Socrates.

As the dark clouds of fascism were descending on Europe, the American-born English poet T.S. Eliot (1888–1965) said in a radio broadcast in February 1937:

> one reason why the lot of the secular reformer or revolutionist seems to me to be the easier is this: that for the most part he conceives of the evils of the world as something external to himself. They are thought of either as completely impersonal, so that there is nothing to alter but machinery: or if there is evil incarnate, it is always incarnate in the other people – a class, a race, the politicians, the bankers, the armament makers, and so forth – never in oneself.

The twentieth century has witnessed an unprecedented number of rampant ideologies failing in self-insight in just the way Eliot described. The Spanish writer José Ortega y Gasset (1883–1955) describes what he ironically calls the 'young master' in a way that reveals how the poisonous weeds of ideology can make barren ground of the human mind and create people who are averse to all suggestions from the outside, deaf to what others say, convinced of the rightness of their own interpretations and considerate of no one but themselves.

Such self-absorption is impotent to cope with nationalism in its most virulent forms. Education and especially religious education can rectify the effects of narrow ideological indoctrination, opening up wide and inclusive prospects of human nature and the human condition. I have already had occasion to comment on the ten states into which Buddhist philosophy analyzes life. The first six of those states – hell, hunger, animality, anger, humanity and heaven – represent life absorbed in the interests of everyday existence. Self-reformation guided by religious education leads to the higher states of learning and realization, where the self is able to reflect on itself. Without this kind of training, the human remains confined to the lower stages of self-absorption and cannot hope to be able to minimize the faults of others while turning a magnifying glass on those of the self.

GALTUNG: The brilliant Hungarian-born British author Arthur Koestler (1905–83) was a communist who turned against communism and one of the six authors of *The God that Failed*. He analyzes his rejection of his former views in his famous essay, 'The Yogi and the Commissar', in which the commissar interprets the whole world, including human and all other forms of life, as a machine that will run as desired if some social reconstruction is performed on it. Needless to say, the commissar himself is the engineer and driver of the machine. To the yogi, however, the commissar's interpretation is all illusion. As T.S. Eliot and Ortega y Gasset have expressed it, the only way to achieve the desired result is by means of self-improvement resulting from self-reflection and the inner dialogue.

Is it not possible to steer a middle way in this case too? Could we not combine the inner and the outer dialogues for the sake of arriving at good solutions to the problems of social formation? Instead of making either–or choices, we must regard the relation between the two as a dialectic that must be consciously steered toward higher levels of personal and social transformation.

Fundamentalism

IKEDA: In his book *Powershift*, the American futurologist Alvin Toffler cites fundamentalism in recent religious revivals as one factor that could make the twenty-first century a Dark Age. He writes:

> While all these religious movements are, of course, different, and frequently clash with one another, and while some are extremist and others not, all of them – Christian or New Age, Judaic or Islamic – are united in one thing – their hostility to secularism, the philosophical base of mass democracy.

As a Buddhist, I do not oppose secularism. I do, however, consider it insufficient. Instead of creating a new world view to replace that of the Middle Ages, the modern period has become an age without a world view. Secularism has advanced no basic proposals for guiding human beings in how they ought to live.

On the other hand, disregarding the benefits of the secular view is mistaken and unproductive. Rationalism is a mainstay of the secular way of life. Instead of adopting a nonrational or antirational stance, we must try to be suprarational; that is, to embrace the rational as well as the many other facets of our being. Religion must create lofty values for humanity and society. Of course, religions that create negative values are truly – to borrow Marx's term – opiates. Together with nationalism, fundamentalism is a pressing issue in the post-ideology age.

GALTUNG: Much thinking on ideology and nationalism applies to religion – including secularism. As has been said, the basic problem is their omissions. Some areas of the subject are blindingly illuminated; others remain in dark shadow. And one may be certain that no light is shed on taboo areas where, as they say, the shoe pinches.

Religious fundamentalists, who are not alone in displaying their attractive points and concealing their faults, are not found only in the Islamic world – as some people in the United States and Western Europe seem to claim.

Fundamentalism tends to legitimize killing for the achievement of some higher goal. In this connection, it is interesting to note that both sides in the Gulf War invoked dogmas of so-called just wars: the Muslims on the basis of the fourth stage of *jihad* (exertion) and some Christians on the basis of the teachings of St Augustine (d. *c*. 605). Both Christians and Muslims truly believed in their causes. And although both killed, the Christians had the more effective killing machine.

Perhaps the best way to deal with fundamentalism – for example, national and religious – is not by denouncing it but by demonstrating and practicing alternatives. An alternative to secular nationalism is globalism and humanism, an all-embracing attachment to the planet Gaea and to all humanity across all the boundaries apparently separating us from one another. Instead of condemning the fundamentalists, we must strengthen truly global organizations that emphasize cooperation based on our common interests rather than conflict based on incompatible values. We must realize the seriousness with which fundamentalists take their own values. The alternative cannot possibly be lack of seriousness, indifference and self-centered unconcern for everything but oneself. The tendency to resort too easily to violence is the problem. The remedy is to show, as Gandhi did, how seriousness and nonviolence go together.

Furthermore, if we are striving for a global civilization, not in the sense of one civilization being imposed on others as the West has, with some success, tried to do, but in the sense of active co-existence, exchange and love; not only for the familiar, nonthreatening self, but also for others because they are different and therefore enriching, then dialogue with fundamentalists is indispensable.

Suppose we could educate our children not just to tolerate, but also to delight in differences and challenges and prepare them to live in a world where diversity is loved as a condition for self-enrichment? Achieving education of this kind and making it possible not merely to study but also actually to learn from other civilizations would be magnificent tasks for schools in general and for universities in particular. We should remember that fundamentalism is a cry yearning to be heard and responded to. It must be heeded.

IKEDA: Norman Cousins (1915–90), the well-known American journalist, with whom I participated in a dialogue, was an ardent advocate of the importance of education, yet said that, not only in the United States but also in many other parts of the world, it has failed because it has generated a mere tribal awareness instead of an awareness of the human race as a whole. A large part of ethnic awareness – or tribal awareness – is an artificial and deliberate product of the process whereby modern ethnic states have come into being. One of our primary educational tasks is to devote attention to finding ways of cultivating an awareness of the whole human race in the minds of the young.

In doing this we must be wary of falling into the error of socialist so-called world-citizens' education and the wretched tragedy of attempts to cultivate communists on the basis of the doctrine of the international proletariat. During the 1920s, Lenin's wife, Nadezhda Krupskaya, (1869–1939) took the initiative in a loudly proclaimed program of encouraging education. Its wretched ending conceals one of the fearsome aspects educational programs can assume. When, in *The State and Revolution*, Lenin said, 'A person who does not want to hear is worse than all the deaf', he revealed an intolerant attitude impermissible in an educator. Educators have great power to alter students profoundly. If fanatic and misguided, they can do psychological damage far worse than physical violence.

GALTUNG: In my mind's eye I can see rows of Pioneers wearing red scarves in Soviet schools or Chinese kindergartens during the years you mention. But I also see children in the United States holding their hands to their hearts as they recite the pledge of allegiance to a flag hanging in the corner of the room. I see Polish children who, now that communism is a thing of the past, pray to their Catholic God. I also see a very, very bad period in Japanese history in the not very distant past. In other words, the communists had no monopoly on indoctrination, nor are they alone in fearing dialogue, a wonderful tool for mutual enrichment.

Educators can indeed – as you say – do psychological damage far worse than physical violence. They can do it not only by glorifying violence, but also by failing to point out how nonviolence can contribute to the elimination of such horrors as colonialism, the Cold War, segregation in the southern United States, Zionist colonization at the expense of the Palestinians and Boer colonization at the expense of the blacks in South Africa. Indoctrination narrows the mind and prepares a person to accept violence as inevitable.

Cultural Relativism

IKEDA: Cultural differences often give rise to friction and strife. Disparate cultural-value criteria are usually at the heart of nationalist problems, which are aggravated by the kind of dominance–submission relationship between two cultures that has characterized Western colonialism. The relativism that has emerged in this century is based on cultural anthropology, in itself a reaction against the condescending attitudes of the colonial mind that considered civilization synonymous with Western civilization and condemned everything else as barbarian. In an admirable manifestation of the Western conscience, cultural relativism insists that all cultures have their own unique values.

But scholarly cultural relativism has not resolved all difficulties. Trade friction between Japan and the United States and between Japan and Europe threatens to degenerate into cultural friction. The French authority on Chinese studies at the University of Paris, Professor Leon Vandermeersch, has made a statement that underscores the partiality with which some Westerners still make cultural judgements. He remarks that Western frustrations can develop into anger when cultural differences threaten the dominant Western position and goes on to say: 'We [Westerners] can readily accept ritual cannibalism among the aborigines of New Guinea, but cannot stand the idea of the Japanese taking only one week of vacation per year.'

Overcoming such misunderstanding and friction requires that we all make ceaseless efforts to avoid emotionalism and elevate the quality of cultural exchanges.

Goethe once commented on the nature of national animosities:

Actually, there is something distinctive about national hatred. You will always find it strongest and fiercest at the lowest cultural levels. But there is a level where it disappears entirely and where, so to speak, people stand above nations and experience the joy or sorrow of their neighboring people as their own. This cultural level is compatible to my nature.

Admission to the level Goethe mentions as compatible is not limited to poetic geniuses. It is open to all.

GALTUNG: The emergence of cultural relativism coincided with decolonialization and the slow realization among Westerners that non-Western people, too, are human beings. Its predecessor was cultural absolutism, in which the preeminent position was afforded to Western culture alone. This attitude still persists. Moreover, the tendency for the relativistic attitude to take the form of passive tolerance instead of active attempts to learn from other cultures unfortunately diminishes the efficacy of cultural relativism.

What comes after cultural relativism? Maybe today's cultural relativism is actually too absolute in the sense of implying that all cultures are equal (even if the idea that some are more equal than others underlies the implication). The time may have come for us to manifest the courage to evaluate cultures without assuming equality.

If we do this, what evaluation do we give to a civilization that, seeing itself as the center of the world, divides the rest into a periphery trying for entry into that center and an outer circle of evil that is eternally shut out and may even be condemned to extermination simply because it wants to remain itself? What can we say of a civilization that regards its own history as universal history that others must repeat by undergoing so-called development or modernization? Unreflective arrogance of this kind should stimulate doubts about Western civilization.

Undeniably, the West has had its shining successes, perhaps most notably in the kind of social differentiation pointed out by thinkers such as Adam Smith (1723–90), Herbert Spencer (1820–1903), Emile Durkheim (1858–1917), and Max Weber (1864–1920); that is, division of labor, division of power, the rule of law, and separation of the person and status of the ruler. Sadly, however, thirst for dominance and a mania for so-called growth tend to overshadow these positive aspects. Its stubborn unwillingness to learn from others and its excessive eagerness to teach, as stated in the missionary command in the New Testament (Matthew XXVIII: 19), leave no room for dialogue. There is no final verse reading 'and have dialogue with all peoples'.

As your quotation from Professor Vandermeersch indicates, Western arrogance is clearly evident in relations with Japan. The problem, as I have had occasion to observe, is actually quite simple. The West – in this instance, specifically the United States – felt itself called upon to elevate Japan to the Western level and to show itself condescendingly, benevolently and paternalistically tolerant while recommending remedies and gently stimulating the other party to admit its own crises and deficiencies. But even this is not the way the West today truly reacts to Japan. The West now has a sneaking suspicion that Japanese culture may indeed be superior in areas where the West has heretofore felt unchallenged. A sense that its culture is secure from fundamental challenge has accounted for Western aggressiveness.

Though Max Weber, an erudite but somewhat provincially Western professor, had promised them the opposite, the West has realized that the Mahayana Buddhist-Confucian tradition may be as productive of economic growth as the Judaeo-Christian tradition. In fact, because of the Japanese people's greater diligence, group discipline and considerateness, it may even be more productive. This shocking contingency was only slowly admitted. And after it was, the West began criticizing all aspects of Japanese culture and structure: the whole patrimony-matrimony including hard work, saving, vacations, housing, corporate structure, low percentage of gross national product devoted to defense, lower consumption, excessively high taxes and so on. Some Westerners consistently assume themselves to be the norm and the Japanese to be deviant or even delinquent. Others, it is true, tried to learn from the Japanese. But in general the West has manifested the missionary tendency to want to bend both Japan and the Japanese people to Western ways.

Finally, I must disagree with the comment by Goethe that you quote. Remarks of this kind are made by Westerners who consider themselves on a higher, not a lower, cultural level than others. Actually it may be a sign of greater hope that I find more curiosity and a greater readiness to learn from others among Westerners who are not of the elite.

IKEDA: You are very strict with Goethe. Since I respect him greatly, I shall attempt a defense. When he speaks of higher and lower levels of civilization, he is not equating the former with European civilization and the latter with all others. The passage I refer to identifies as low-level civilizations those characterized by national evil. His high-level civilizations are those that empathize with the happiness and unhappiness of their neighbors. This standard indicates the universal significance of the cultivated human personality.

Because they are relative, it is difficult to establish value-criteria among cultures. Nonetheless, only the most gravely misguided condone the actions of a Hitler or a Stalin. The general emotional reaction to them is unfavorable. There are, however, other phenomena to which the human emotional response is universally favorable. I believe the character of the true citizen of the world, like Goethe, is one of those phenomena. As human concerns in the current age grow increasingly international, the world-citizen outlook should be emulated by all.

Cultural relativism should be more than relative. Of course, it must not be allowed to become bogged down at the state you describe as passive tolerance combined with unwillingness to learn. It is always bad to remain content with what one has, no matter how good it is, and lazily to see no advantage in becoming richer through the acquisition of diversity and abundance of knowledge and experience. While remaining aware of cultural relativism, we must pursue the universal elements in human nature. Understanding values that are universal throughout human history is helpful in encouraging respect for the dignity of the individual. In connection with the search for the universal, we have much to learn from such global citizens as Socrates and Goethe.

GALTUNG: I interpret Goethe to be talking about fierce national hatreds at the lowest social levels and about more globally aware elites who transcend national affiliations. In my experience throughout the world, however, I have found intense, even pathological, nationalism low down on the social scale, particularly in the kind of *Lumpenproletariat* we see today among Serbs and Croats, as well as among Muslims, in the former Yugoslavia and also in elites who consider themselves the bearers of national interests. The elites send the lower classes into battle to kill and be killed. Middle classes are, by and large, more globally oriented. They spin webs of affiliation around the world; they create nongovernmental organizations and transnational companies. They prefer a world where they can travel all over, to satisfy their curiosity and do business to make a profit. Of course, there are luminary exceptions from all classes, like the two you mention, Goethe and Socrates, to whom I should like to add Shakyamuni; Confucius, a contemporary of Socrates; and Soseki Natsume (1867–1916), one of my own favorite Japanese authors.

The expansion of the middle classes, pushing the other two classes further to the margins of society, is in my view a great source of hope. Our basic task is to stimulate dialogue in the name of creating a nonviolent world ethos. You have done this masterfully in 'Mahayana Buddhism and Twenty-first Century Civilization'. How do you think this attempt can become part of a world ethos not merely for a few exceptional people, but for the billions of us ordinary human beings as well?

IKEDA: As a Buddhist, I believe that religion – and, more precisely, a religion that serves the needs of humanity and emphasizes those elements that differentiate human beings from other creatures – holds the key to the achievement of a world free of violence and to the success of dialogues for the sake of attaining that goal. In commenting on a speech I made at Harvard, the religious scholar

Professor Harvey Cox expressed hopes for the restoration of a global religious spirit but remarked on such negative aspects of religion as fanaticism and prejudice and preserved a prudent attitude toward the 'Age of Religion'. Certainly I respect his opinion as an earnest expression of his many years of research and experience.

I, too, am fully aware of cautionary views on religion in general and have myself often spoken on their merits and demerits. This is why, at Harvard, I said that serving as a basis for the rehabilitation of humanity is a mainstay of the role Buddhism will play in the twenty-first century. I spoke of the necessity of religion as an encourager and supporter of active living in search of the good and the valuable. This is the inherent meaning of a religion that serves the needs of humanity.

Religions tend to lapse into rigid, authoritarian dogma that, instead of increasing human strength and wisdom, leads the world into evil and folly. While invoking the concepts of the American philosopher John Dewey (1859–1952), I emphasized the importance of religion in order to warn against such dogma. Because of dogmatic approaches, it is difficult for religion to become a human ethos. Although an enthusiastic supporter of our movement, Professor Cox is so strongly impressed by the countless human sacrifices made in the name of religion that he doubts the religious element has the power to appeal to the world's majority. Certainly its outlook for the twenty-first century is dark, unless religion can extricate itself from the entangling karma of its history. This is why religion has reached an apparently hopeless impasse.

Our movement for a contemporary religious revolution and a renaissance of values constitutes a challenge to this impasse. The Soka Gakkai International advocates a fundamental revolution in opposition to the kind of religious dogmatism and authoritarianism that dominate and subjugate human beings. Undeniably, work in the name of a religion that serves the needs of humanity is difficult in unprecedented ways. But the Soka Gakkai is already spreading in 150 countries. This achievement inspires in me a certain amount of pride and confidence.

United Nations: Reorganization

IKEDA: The Gulf crisis showed that the United Nations can reach agreement within itself in order to deal with something like the Iraqi invasion of Kuwait. It also pointed up certain areas – such as relations between the General Assembly and the Security Council and the competence of the secretary-general – that, as the UN's role becomes increasingly important, require serious attention. At a United Nations armament conference held in Kyoto in 1991,

Vladimir F. Petrovskii, then Soviet vice-minister for foreign affairs, now head of the United Nations in Geneva, said he felt the future would be an age in which responsibility for keeping the peace devolves fully on the United Nations. On the other hand, the Iranian UN representative asked what the Security Council had done to keep the peace by preventing the crisis in the Gulf from degenerating into war.

Today the world is in need of wise ideas and wise actions. Maurice Bertrand, a former member of the United Nations Joint Inspection Unit, has said that now, after the end of the Cold War – or World War III – we require a third-generation international structure. In other words, the world has outgrown the United Nations in its present form. Various proposals – including your own – have already been advanced for its reorganization.

GALTUNG: In my book *United Nations; United Peoples*, I explore ten proposals for reorganization. Some of them deal with the political United Nations, its most familiar aspect, including the General Assembly, the Security Council and the member states. Others involve the professional UN; that is, its specialized agencies. Still others are concerned with what I call the peoples' United Nations. Here I shall confine myself to the first category.

In spite of all the reasons it advanced for its invasion of Kuwait on 2 August 1990, at the time of the Gulf War Iraq faced, practically speaking, unanimous condemnation from the United Nations. There were good and fairly obvious reasons for this. As constituted today, the United Nations is a trade union of governments with shared interests in inviolable borders. This does not, however, justify as an adequate response massive attacks killing and wounding perhaps close to 500,000 persons, mostly civilians. I regard the Gulf War as a capitulation on the part of the United Nations Security Council and a tragedy of considerable magnitude. Offers of negotiations were rejected. The United States and the United Kingdom applied enormous pressure to win their aims. And acting in accordance with Article 12 of the UN Charter, the Security Council monopolized security affairs without reference to the General Assembly. In spite of all this, the war was *not* a United Nations operation: it was only a coalition legitimized by the Security Council.

In my view, membership of the Security Council should be increased from 25 to 30 in order to enable all parts of the world to express their opinions. The idea of permanent-member status may be retained, but it should be expanded to include Japan, India and certain other countries. The right of veto granted to some members, however, must be abolished at once. No small group of states should be empowered to decide so much for so many with such potentially fatal consequences. Empowerment of this kind is a remnant of feudalism and is completely incompatible with global democracy. Moreover, as a study of Security Council vetoes shows, it serves no useful purpose. Such vetoes only manage to delay programs for a few years.

In addition, I argue for a change in the dues structure. No country's contribution should be assessed at more than 10 per cent of the UN's income. Even 10 per cent may be too high. The financial shock to the organization is earth-shaking when a nation paying dues amounting to 25 per cent of the total budget decides to withdraw. A loss of only 10 per cent would amount to no more than a minor tremor. Of course, members must be permitted to withdraw. Making membership eternally binding only heightens tensions. Furthermore, countries which do withdraw will tend to return.

I doubt the soundness of keeping the United Nations headquarters permanently in Manhattan, New York, the United States, or in any one place. Fifty years in one spot should certainly suffice. At least, I think a decision to change location should be made before the year 2000. I recommend relocating the headquarters to a very populous part of the world where many languages are spoken: for instance Hong Kong, if suitable real estate is available there by 1997. Relocation of this kind would not only better reflect the realities of the present-day globe, but would also wean the whole world and the West in particular from the notion that the West is and remains the sole world center. After 50 years in East Asia, the headquarters could relocate to, perhaps, Africa.

Finally, I suggest that the concept of intervention be brought up to date. The United Nations came into being in an age when intervention necessarily meant military intervention. After all, the organization is a product of one of the most gruesome wars in human history and bears the imprint of the epoch of its genesis. Even today, its members are trying to repeat the acts of their big-power predecessors. As I have already said, however, for our own time I recommend nonviolent, international peace brigades made up of both young and old, men and women, trained in mediation and conflict-resolution in general. They should be armed only with the kinds of protective equipment stipulated in Chapter 6 of the United Nations Charter, the section dealing with peacekeeping forces. Numbering thousands and tens of thousands, they should be the new heroes of the post-military age and should fully understand their missions. The presence of a hundred thousand such people in former Yugoslavia might have prevented all the bloodshed. But in Somalia, UN military intervention caused the first war of liberation against the United Nations. In such cases, idealism is considerably more realistic than so-called military realism.

IKEDA: In this time of violent change, the United Nations itself and the Security Council in particular have arrived at a dramatic turning point. In 1992 the Security Council unanimously approved dispatching a multinational force, headed by the United States, to ensure the safety of deliveries of humanitarian aid to Somalia. Because of its humanitarian nature, few objected to this move. But the subsequent peace-enforcing activities, the first in the history of peacekeeping, reached an impasse.

In dealing with the numerous ethnic uprisings now occurring in many parts of the world, however, the United Nations must react. The kinds of intervention open to it are a topic of heated debate. The internal nature of most of these conflicts makes responding to them very difficult. The United Nations can no longer abide by its former policy of nonintervention in the domestic affairs of member nations. By adopting compulsory measures to ensure the safety of humanitarian-aid operations, the organization has intervened in territorial (internal) affairs, thus opening up new directions for future actions. Secretary-General Boutros Boutros-Ghali stimulated considerable debate when, in a report entitled 'An Agenda for Peace', he brought up the idea of heavily armed peace-enforcement forces that could be dispatched to an area without the consent of the parties to a conflict there, in order to force the cessation of hostilities. This indicates the independence with which the United Nations is now willing to deal with difficulties arising in the post-Cold War world.

Under such circumstances, to prevent our being dragged into unforeseeable quagmires, we must recall the fundamental and essential role the United Nations was created to play. In all instances, we must be wary of rushing into things.

I always consider the basic role of the UN to lie in the soft-power realm of evolving systems and rules to harmonize the activities of its member states. These systems and the rules arising from them are the diametric opposites of military hard power. I agree with Professor Joseph Nye of Harvard when he describes soft power as the power not of competition, but of cooperation. The power of cooperation must be the foundation of the desperately needed new world order.

Today many people criticize the excessive weight afforded to opinions of Security Council permanent members. Solving this problem requires the creation of a new system – a global Security Council. Eliminating the veto alone will be insufficient. The roles of the General Assembly and the secretary-general must be reinforced to prevent excessively arbitrary action on the part of the Security Council. The United Nations celebrates its fiftieth birthday in 1995. It would be an excellent thing to hold a world summit in order to work out a variety of proposals for reorganization before the year 2000.

GALTUNG: I agree, but much is at stake. First, as we have said several times, the limitation of violence is essential. Less obviously, mere legitimization by the Security Council, as was attempted by Resolution 678 in the case of the Gulf War, does not cause these limitations on violence to vanish. Furthermore, there are limits to the legal paradigm – so dear to the present secretary-general – whereby rules are made and violators of those rules are punished 'with all necessary means'. In the case of the Gulf War, the means took the form of economic sanctions, as in the case of former Yugoslavia, too. But probably Saddam Hussein undertook the war out of a desire to display courage and to seek dignity and honor for standing up against all the countries that historically have humiliated Iraq. In a sense, therefore, the war served his purposes. In former Yugoslavia, punitive measures have only strengthened the more fundamentalist segments of the population, intensifying traumas that have already almost set world records. I should like a summit meeting to be both willing and able to address such matters, which, though perhaps outside their usual competencies, must be approached with open minds. The present legalistic, punishment-oriented United Nations fails, among other reasons, because it has an unrealistic approach to very complicated phenomena.

United Nations: Development and Environmental Protection

IKEDA: I know you have an interesting idea that the United Nations should be a bicameral organization with an upper and a lower house. Representation in the upper house should be, as in the General Assembly today, limited to one person, with one vote, from each member state. Representation in the lower house – the Peoples' Assembly – should be proportional to member-state population.

World conditions today are very different from those that prevailed in 1945, when the United Nations officially came into being. The environment was not a major issue then. The founders of the organization were only vaguely aware of many of the problems that loom large on our horizon now. For these reasons, the United Nations Economic and Social Council and its ancillary organizations for trade and development, environmental planning, population control and developmental planning are insufficient to the task of dealing with contemporary difficulties.

This is why I recommend strengthening the organization by dividing its responsibilities between two independent bodies. The peacekeeping United Nations should become the Security United Nations. Responsibilities for the environment, economy, development, population, food and human rights should be remitted to a second United Nations for Development and the Environment. Seventy per cent of the overall budget and staff should go to the second body, which should be devoted to humane activities and aid for developing nations.

I propose a new organization instead of a mere revamping of the Economic and Social Council because of the need for strength and international decision-making capabilities. Such a new organization would be able to cope with global problems in a precise, yet flexible, manner.

GALTUNG: Since I am very much in favor of strengthening all its nonmilitary capacities, I welcome the idea of making the United Nations a better instrument for providing development and environmental protection. But I am not convinced that establishing two independent bodies, as you suggest, is a good idea. Their success would depend on how independent the two were from each other.

There are arguments in favor of the concept. It might be good to separate the hard United Nations from the soft; that is, the punishing father in the form of the security organization from the gentle compassionate mother in the form of the development and environmental organization. The activities of the hard body could not be laid at the door of the soft body. (A similar argument was once advanced to justify the separation of state and church.)

But the idea of keeping everything together in the center of world governance that the United Nations may one day become seems even more persuasive. Much can be said for holism and for a General Assembly that is not only permitted but also encouraged to pronounce on any issue under the sun and for UN agencies that deal with, practically speaking, everything. Joint action is sometimes needed. Peacekeeping operations are an example of the need. In the twenty-first century, when environmental catastrophes strike – particularly those related to scarce water – such operations will become increasingly numerous.

Consequently, I would prefer to see the secretary-general surrounded by a moderate number of capable under-secretaries, each responsible for a key aspect of the whole United Nations system. Instead of being detached from them, the softer functions, too, should be used preventively so as to make the harder functions redundant.

I must hasten to add, however, that at present, in spite of a certain limited potential in that direction, the United Nations demonstrates little holism. A personal anecdote may illustrate what I mean. During the 1970s, when the Third World was 'in' and the superpowers 'out' because the Vietnam War and the labor camps of the Gulag had illegitimized them, I was expert consultant and adviser

to ten United Nations agencies. (This all changed in the
Reagan–Bush years, when the United States regained control of
the organization.) During 1975 and 1976, I was working on a
theory of technological transfer for the United Nations Council on
Trade and Development (UNCTAD) and on an international
study on schizophrenia for the World Health Organization (WHO).
Both organizations are located in Geneva, where parking is scarce.
For speedy transit from one office to the other, I commuted by easy-
to-park scooter from the UNCTAD building, next to the Palais
des Nations, to the WHO building, a couple of kilometers away.

At UNCTAD it was considered desirable to transfer almost
limitless technology from the First to the Third World, preferably
at no cost to the Third World. At WHO, on the other hand, the
primary concern was not money but costs in terms of mental
health, because schizophrenia rates are at least ten times higher,
and the disorder more serious and long-lasting, in countries where
technological development is advanced. My scooter, which impressed
no one in terms of technology, was the only vehicle of contact
between these two divergent interpretations of costs. Isolation
between United Nations sub-organizations persists today. Though
diversity is good, I suspect that insufficient coordination hinders
the kind of fruitful dialogues that could make that diversity beneficial.

IKEDA: Many proposals for the reorganization of the United Nations
are said to be under discussion. The secretary-general has apparently
convened a committee of representatives from 14 nations to consider
plans for basic reform.

But, at present at any rate, the outlook for the solution of environmental and developmental problems is none too bright. As a
result of the United Nations Conference on the Environment and
Development (UNCED, or Earth Summit), held in Rio de Janeiro
in 1992, the United Nations established a new bureau of policy
coordination and sustainable development, which includes a
committee on the nature of such development. From now on these
organizations will be in charge of the Earth's environment problems.

Although everything is still uncertain, implementing decisions
taken at UNCED is likely to be difficult. The so-called Agenda 21[*]

---

[*] In June 1992, the United Nations Conference of the Environment and Development
(UNCED, the 'Earth Summit') was held in Rio de Janeiro and adopted an action
plan for the protection of the environment. This was named 'Agenda 21'. It
proposes: to change 'unsustainable patterns of production and consumption, particularly of the industrialized countries which do not reflect adequate concern for
environmental conservation and rehabilitation'; to raise money for development
programs by increasing overseas development aid (ODA) from 0.35 to 0.7 per cent
of gross domestic product (GDP); to protect forest and sea resources; to transfer
appropriate technology to developing countries.

is supposed to be a prescription for dealing with these issues, but as yet no one knows where to begin putting it into practice. Such complications only hint at the vast scale of our environmental difficulties.

The current worldwide economic slump can hamper implementation by dampening enthusiasm for environmental protection. Unless the United Nations comes up with some very bold ideas, global environmental protection is unlikely to make much progress.

Whereas in general I am in agreement with your idea of keeping everything together in the center of world governance, I am concerned about how we can reach the point where such a thing is possible. Not long ago, Mr Peter Hansen, then executive director of the Commission on Global Governance, visited Soka Gakkai headquarters for a talk. His is an independent organization for the development of new systems and the establishment of new global values. He called on us in the hope that Soka Gakkai can contribute to his Commission's work.

Now that the Cold War has ended, security concern has shifted from the narrow concept of protection from foreign invasions to the much wider notion of global security, including such factors as environmental destruction, economic gaps and instability. I am very interested in the proposals of the Commission on Global Governance in connection with realizing these concepts of global values and security.

GALTUNG: I had the honor of producing one of the background papers for that commission. In it I made detailed proposals for both a United Nations Peoples' Assembly (UNPA) with one, preferably directly, elected representative for each million inhabitants, and a United Nations Corporate Assembly (UNCA) for transnational corporations. The whole world would benefit from bilateral and trilateral dialogues involving the General Assembly, UNPA and UNCA. The nation state, capital and civil society* must be brought together, because today governments run too much of the show alone.

United Nations: Civic-participation System

IKEDA: Undeniably some of the United Nations' limitations arise from the nature of the organization as a union of sovereign states. State interests take precedence and hinder the adoption of humanity-wide viewpoints in decision-making. To correct this failing, concerns

---

* Civil society: people and their associations, such as kinship and friendship, neighborhood and voluntary organizations, as distinct from the state/bureaucracy and capital/corporatism.

for the entire human race must be allowed to come first in both the structure and the operations of the United Nations.

The language of its charter recognizes that the UN ought to be an organization devoted to the interests of both nations and human beings, first when it says, 'We the peoples of the United Nations' and later when it mentions 'our respective governments'. Today, however, governments monopolize much of the organization. Peoples have little chance to make themselves heard. This is especially unfair at a time when nongovernmental organizations – private citizens – are assuming roles of increasing importance in world affairs. Surely such worldwide problems as environmental pollution must be resolved on an all-humanity level and not from the standpoint of state interests. For this reason, I agree with your idea of creating what you call the United Nations Peoples' Assembly to rank with the current General Assembly, which is a gathering of governmental representatives.

Of course, I am implying neither that governments are always in the wrong nor that ordinary people infallibly make wise decisions. But I am of one opinion with you when you say we can build a better world if governments and ordinary people cooperate. Do you have other concrete proposals for introducing into the United Nations a civic-participation system to give voice to the will of the peoples of the world? What would be the composition of your United Nations Peoples' Assembly?

GALTUNG: As has been pointed out, modern society consists of three components: the state, which sometimes makes economic plans; corporations, which administer markets; and civil society, suspended somewhere between the other two. In democracies, civil society exercises some control over the state through electoral influences on party-cratic or parliament-ocratic institutions – mainly the latter. But the only influence the general populace has over corporations is the negative one of buying less. By and large, the people play no positive part in guiding the flow of new products.

In international society, the situation is even worse. States are organized into the United Nations and other functional and regional organizations. International civil society blossoms in thousands of peoples' organizations, which governments condescendingly refer to as 'nongovernmental organizations' (NGOs). This terminology is like calling a woman a 'nonman' or a government a 'nonpeople organization'. The problem, however, is that the United Nations is in fact a non-people organization because it is not accountable to any body of world citizens. Each delegation is responsible to its home government only. Its responsibility does not extend further than its own government and is indeed limited to foreign-policy activities. In other words, accountability is too slight, too indirect and too fragmentary.

That is why I, on many occasions and along with many others, have advocated a United Nations Peoples' Assembly to serve as a second chamber, acting parallel with the General Assembly. To be more specific, let me cite three of the several available concrete models for this second chamber.

First, existing organizations with consultative status in relation to part of the UN system could be invited to deliberate the United Nations' agenda before each session. They could make use of the General Assembly hall during the summer months, when it is not in use.

Second, a systematic survey could be made of international peoples' organizations to select members of the UNPA. Criteria for selection might include such considerations as whether the group in question elects officials democratically, whether it functions in all the major regions of the world, whether it demonstrates basic concern for fundamental United Nations issues and whether it possesses a minimum of proven organizational stability. Nations, some of which may fail to satisfy these conditions, could then take peoples' organizations as models for emulation. Each body, from vast ones like the International Consumers Union, the Red Cross and the Red Crescent to small but important groups in the fields of peace, development and the environment, should have one vote. Humanity looks better viewed through the perspective of such peaceful organizations than it does when seen through nation states armed to the teeth.

Third, members of the Peoples' Assembly might be directly elected from the close to 190 United Nations member states. The number is constantly increasing. Representation should be direct and based on the impressive All India and European Union elections. With more than 5.5 billion human beings on Earth, assigning one representative for each million inhabitants and ensuring that all member states have a minimum of one representative would produce a UNPA with about 5,700 members – unwieldy but not impossible.

Ideally, the meetings of this second chamber should be held at the same time as those of the General Assembly; and the two should have overlapping agendas. In the event of disagreement between them, decisions could be postponed; or a joint-committee system like the one employed in the United States Congress could be used to resolve disputes. This would enable one assembly to balance and correct the other. In the light of the benefits promised by the bicameral arrangement, I eagerly recommend that a second United Nations Assembly be established. It might be a good idea to try all three of the models outlined above, in the order given.

IKEDA: I agree that something like your Peoples' Assembly should be a major aim of reform but suggest that it can be best attained, gradually, by taking advantage of the strengths of nongovernmental organizations. At present, the United Nations Charter limits the participation of such organizations to conferences on the level of the Economic and Social Council. In view of their vigorous activities, this limitation is unnatural. I recommend taking steps to permit NGOs to cooperate at the level of the Security Council and the General Assembly.

I must add my belief in the urgent need to reinforce the role of the Economic and Social Council. In the journal *Foreign Affairs*, Secretary-General Boutros Boutros-Ghali proposed introducing into the council high-level mechanisms to link all its organizations and enable it to respond continually and on a timely basis to new developments in its realm of competency. If this reform is implemented, nongovernmental organizations would have a greatly expanded field in which to demonstrate their strengths. Indeed, in the same *Foreign Affairs* article the secretary-general expressed the hope that in the future NGOs will make many contributions to the United Nations in various ways. Over 1,000 of them are said to be working with the UN now to attain similar goals. Secretary-General Ghali, of whose future leadership we all have great expectations, urges that sincere attention be paid to these NGOs at the level of international organizations and international society.

GALTUNG: Certainly a step-by-step approach must be taken to create a UNPA, which will not come into being easily. Still, we need a global democracy, and the UNPA is the way to achieve it. The sum of all national democracies does not constitute a global democracy. I agree with you that corporations must not be left out of the picture. Perhaps I believe more in long-lasting dialogues leading to new ideas and consensus than in short debates entailing few ideas and ending in decisions reached by means of voting, in which there are winners and losers. One approach does not, however, exclude the other.

United Nations: Japan's International Contributions

IKEDA: A great bone of domestic contention in relation to Japanese contributions to international affairs has been participation by our self-defense forces in United Nations peacekeeping operations. In a speech delivered at the beginning of 1992, I said that instead of being narrowly obsessed with this one topic, we ought to discover what broad contributions Japan can make to the creation and maintenance of peace throughout the world.

One area in which Japanese money and technical know-how could be very useful is the protection of the Asian environment. In its haste to develop economically, Asia has become one of the world's leading environment-polluting regions. You have said that the key to solving our environmental dilemma is not money but the uses to which we put the latest technology. Many nations would welcome infusions of Japanese environmental-protection and energy-conservation technology, which are on a par with the best in the world. Nations have the right to develop economically. We must respect that right. At the same time, all nations, including Japan, must contribute to the creation of a new system of coexistence for the sake of the planet on which all human development and prosperity depend.

GALTUNG: To begin with, a minor matter: it might be an idea for the Japanese to change their style a little in order to improve communications. Japan often acts silently, to achieve its ends without any song or dance. This can be a very good thing. For example, at the end of the 1980s Japan financed the Committee of Eminent Persons for the reorganization of the United Nations. Very few people are aware of the excellent work Japan does in this way. There are cases, however, when more skillful public relations would improve Japan's international reputation. In his book *Japan Unmasked*, the diplomat Ichiro Kawasaki observed that Japanese participants in international organizations operate on the basis of the 'three s's': smiles, sleep and silence. The smile may be endearing, but sleeping – as the Japanese do successfully on suburban commuting trains – is ineffective, even counterproductive, in conferences, where it can easily be interpreted as lack of interest. And though not actually remaining silent all the time, even Japanese with a perfect command of the English language are rarely eloquent in international meetings. If heard at all, they frequently come across as serious but somewhat boring and pedantic.

Setting that aside, I think the idea of affording top priority to environmental protection is excellent. But how is Japan, a country that has already consumed tremendous amounts of marine resources and forests, including rainforests in the Third World in general and Southeast Asia in particular, going to achieve this? A negative measure would be to curtail consumption of such resources. A more positive option would be to encourage a return to local use of local resources. This would not only directly concern the local population with whatever mess is created, but also perhaps influence conditions in order to prevent pollution and depletion. This would be preventative medicine of a sort. Still another possibility would involve curative medicine; that is, introducing advanced technology from outside to clean up messes that have already been made.

I admit to skepticism here. For example, suppose Japan brings in advanced equipment to clean up oil spills or soil contamination. How much pollution would the clean-up equipment and its transport from point A to point B generate? Could the pollutants extracted in the cleaning process be successfully disposed of? If they could, at what cost to the environment would this be?

I have yet to see a completely convincing budget for a total clean-up project of this kind. Moreover, relying on such operations might create another kind of dependency on Japan.

By far the most important contribution Japan can make is to use its wealth to support international civil society by encouraging peoples' organizations, promoting and sponsoring culture and cultural understanding, and propagating new concepts of defense based on a positive interpretation of Article 9 of the Japanese constitution.

Above all, Japan should divest itself of its present client status in relation to the United States, thus setting a model of nonaggressive autonomy. Japan could become a first-rate peacemaker, emulating and far surpassing neutral Switzerland. When conflicts arise, Japan should be a venue for negotiations among all parties, even if it displeases the United States. No matter whether the US or Japan is on top, Japan should abide by the logic of peace, not the logic of world hegemony.

It is time for Japan to become independent and to grow up. Now that the Cold War threat is long gone – if indeed it ever existed – continued bondage to the security-treaty system (called AMPO in Japanese) can only lead to increased tension, making Japan an accessory to a major conflict instead of a third party, an honest broker, generously available to all. The time may have come to phase out that security treaty and replace it with peace attained by peaceful means in a multilateral setting. Of course, the United Nations is of primary importance in connection with this step.

IKEDA: You make some telling points. Today large numbers of Japanese travel overseas. At home, everyone talks of internationalization and Japan's contributions to global society. Yet I wonder to what extent Japanese opinions are accepted in other countries. There is nothing wrong with our nation's being affluent, but the nouveau-riche attitude should be taboo. The important thing for the Japanese to do is to win respect throughout the world. The roots of internationalization do not go deep in Japan, an insular nation in every respect, where attitudes have traditionally swung back and forth between xenophobia and worship of the foreign.

Your comment that 'Japan could become a first-rate peacemaker' strikes home because it makes us realize how much growing up and maturing we must do and how much more diligently we must refine our diplomatic abilities. In connection with Japanese shortcomings in communication skills, perhaps attention should be called to our dislike of direct facial expression of emotions. People from other countries often comment on our deadpan ways.

Be that as it may, undeniably we must grow up. We ought to be modest, never arrogant, and, as you wisely suggest, must promote culture and cultural understanding while propagating the spirit of Article 9 of the Japanese constitution.

GALTUNG: Some time ago, I suggested to the Tokyo metropolitan government that Tokyo be made the peace capital of the world and provide conflicting parties with personnel skilled in conflict-negotiations. I firmly believe that there is no substitute for creative conflict-reduction and that preventative therapy is much better than more-or-less curative steps taken after a conflict has broken out and, through its violent manifestations, has inflicted hard-to-heal emotional wounds.

In this connection, steeped as it is in the nonviolent Buddhist tradition, Soka University could make a major contribution by providing personnel. Other Japanese universities, too, could be drawn upon: the International Christian University, Chuo University and Meiji Gakuin University, to name only a few. Perhaps a consortium could be established to train conflict mediators. Much needs to be done, and Japan has not only economic but also, far more importantly, intellectual and spiritual resources to draw upon.

The Haves and the Have-nots

IKEDA: Undeniably, industrialized nations exploit and pollute the environment beyond their own boundaries. Their developmental structure imposes huge cumulative obligations on developing nations, who must ravage their resources in order simply to pay interest on their debts. In the light of this lamentable situation, co-operation between the haves and have-nots is unlikely.

To improve conditions, wealthy nations must do away with political and economic structures that exploit developing nations and work to create a new system ensuring prosperity for all. Solving the problem of the have and have-not nations – that is, the so-called North–South problem – is most urgent.

GALTUNG: The United Nations Rio de Janeiro Earth Summit was by and large a disaster, largely because of procrastination on the

CHOOSE PEACE

part of the United States. Many countries were so cowed that they willingly modified draft conventions merely to prevent the United States from walking out or becoming a minority of one. Then too, no doubt some nations concealed their own procrastination by hiding behind the United States, on which they confidently relied to cling to its wasteful lifestyle and to sabotage important climate and species-preservation instruments.

Environmental issues have only come to the forefront as a result of the work of peoples' organizations. Very little would have been done in the ecological field had not organizations such as Greenpeace mobilized public opinion. Governments and corporations have only acted because civil society has shamed them into it.

In one respect, however, UNCED did succeed: it managed to move environmental issues from peoples' organizations into governmental ministries and corporation boardrooms and it forced government and business experts and intellectuals to act, or at least react. Be that as it may, peoples' organizations must not abandon these issues or rely on nations and corporations – the worst polluters – to behave rationally. To do so is to invite catastrophe.

UNCED might be compared to a meeting of slave-holders trying to find a way not to abolish slavery, but to promote sustainable slavery. To continue the analogy, under the arrangement devised by the slave-holders, even non-slave states demanded their share of the profits of the trade. In environmental terms, such profit would amount to the slave-holder's share of world depletion and pollution at home.

What is to be done? Certain conditions must be imposed. First, we must concentrate on more local development of smaller economic cycles and a greener (or more Buddhist, in the Schumacher sense) approach in the form of economies geared to satisfying basic human needs. This is the only system that safeguards the needs of nonhuman nature too. It does so by making the preservation of the environment a vested interest of local inhabitants. A transnational approach would permit outsiders to arrive, take whatever resources they want and depart, leaving behind only depletion and pollution. The shorter the depletion-pollution cycle, the sooner will the victims mobilize in self-defense.

Second, we require more direct democracy, in the sense not only of referenda on environmental issues, but also of the right to express concerns on given issues, to demonstrate publicly and to act without being threatened or even killed by governmental and business agents. A basic element of democracy is the right to engage in antipolitics. Direct dialogue not just between capital and the state, as is the case in Japan, but also between peoples' organizations and assemblies of corporations would be useful.

Third, we must encourage greater South–South cooperation, as suggested in the excellent Report of the South Commission (*The Challenge of the South*), chaired by Julius Nyerere, former president of Tanzania. In the past, the Third World has unsuccessfully tried two different policies: substituting local products for imported ones by independently developing secondary and tertiary sectors in each country; and improving terms of trade with the First World by means of many UNCTAD conferences and similar meetings. But local elites have generally preferred imported First World products, and the First World has been uninterested in promoting serious local production in and competition from the Third World.

The method of the South Commission is simple: let us work together, by means of massive student exchanges to decrease academic dependence on the First World, our own schemes for avoiding the hard-currency trap, and so on. The idea of the South's taking its development into its own hands inspires hope. The same applies to Eastern Europe and the former Soviet Union. Ideally, the Third World and the former socialist world should join forces.

IKEDA: The points enumerated by Ernst Schumacher make a fresh impact on us Japanese. His major work, *Small is Beautiful*, has great and no doubt constantly increasing cultural significance extending beyond the economic realm.

Schumacher's ideas on Buddhist economy interest me greatly, especially his three definitions of the role of labor: the provision of opportunities for human beings to manifest and improve their abilities; the stimulus to abandon self-centered attitudes by working together with others on a single task; and the production of property and services necessary for a decent way of life. These definitions indicate a sharp departure from established notions of the supreme importance of efficiency and of the subjugation of human beings to material things. Schumacher's attitude is vividly displayed in his book's subtitle: *A Study of Economics as if People Mattered.*

The strikingly negative emphasis placed by many sects on the supramundane has undeniably led many Buddhists to despise all worldly matters, including of course economics. Under such circumstances, it was virtually impossible for anything like a Buddhist economics to emerge. This is why Schumacher's basically European approach could have a valuable impact on the revitalization of Buddhism.

GALTUNG: Yes, it could. And, since work ennobles people when they act for the sake of self-realization and communal social usefulness, we should get the young and the old, children and retirees, involved as well. In this way children could benefit without being exploited. But for this to happen, we must open up such less

productive sectors of the economy as reproduction of nature, care
of the sick and lonely, and cultural and spiritual activities. The task
is immensely challenging.

An Approach to Global Problems

IKEDA: If current trends continue unchecked, the world's population
will reach 10 billion by the middle of the twenty-first century.
Together with poverty and threats to the environment, the population
issue constitutes a closely interwoven, tripartite global dilemma of
staggering complexity. Now that the East–West conflict has come
to an end, we must convert the trillion dollars spent annually on
defense during the Cold War years to solving such problems as these.

Generating energy to satisfy long-term world demands will be
difficult. Nonetheless, we have relied too long on limited, highly
polluting fossil fuels. At present, the 20 per cent of the global
population living in industrialized nations accounts for 80 per cent
of overall energy consumption. This situation is becoming intolerable. But altering it will require changes in living styles that many
of the world's affluent are unwilling to accept. We must address
these global problems before it is too late.

GALTUNG: During the Earth Summit, proposals were made to
solve some of these problems by attempting to make lifestyles in
the North, particularly in the First World, more rational in the sense
of making them compatible with diminishing resources. The United
States rejected this as violating freedom of choice. The important
point, of course, is that freedom of choice of lifestyle in the North
reduces freedom of choice in the South. Voltaire made this point
eloquently in *Traité sur la tolérance*, but it was somehow missed by
the Bush administration.

The English economist Thomas Malthus (1766–1834) warned
that although population increases by geometric progression, the
food supply increases only by arithmetic progression. The direction
in which we are headed today makes Malthus look like an optimist.
Population seems to be increasing geometrically, but production
of food has actually decreased because of the synergistic effects of
desertification, soil erosion, reduction in species diversity, toxic
pollutants, climate changes and damage caused by depletion of the
ozone layer. UNCED did nothing significant to halt these trends.
It only articulated them.

At some point, however, massive popular protest may save us.
Moreover, the great diversity of available alternative energy sources
– solar, wind, wave, geothermal and aquathermal power, biomass
and so on – makes it hard for me to believe that rationality will not

some day get the upper hand and force highly irrational Western nations to abandon their dependence on nonrenewable fossil fuels. Of course, alternative sources will have to be used in combination since none of them is sufficient on its own. In spite of its folly, however, at the present time burning petroleum remains the so-called modern thing to do.

I am afraid that our world system is too militarized for us to be able to expect quick results from what is referred to as the peace dividend. Many factors combine to justify pessimism in this area. First, the United States, the biggest military spender of all, is also the greatest debtor in human history. Most of the money saved by reducing the defense budget – and so far this has been very little and may well be overshadowed by military expenses concealed in the opaque federal budget – will be used to pay off some of the government's budget deficit in order for the United States to continue as a viable nation. Though the Cold War may be over, most of the big defense spenders are now so rapidly becoming involved in other major conflicts that they may soon begin rearming instead of disarming. The European Union could be on a collision course with a future Russian Union or could join the United States against the Muslim world in general and the Turkish conglomerate in particular: the Economic Cooperation Organization (ECO) countries, with a combined population of 300 million and 10 million square kilometers comprising Turkey, Iran, Pakistan, Afghanistan and the six Central Asian Islamic republics of the former Soviet Union. The conflict in the former Yugoslavia could stimulate such development. In addition, a policy of using military means to guarantee free trade and access to raw materials could lead to collisions with the Third World. Perhaps for a while the haves and have-nots must go their separate ways.

There is much to learn from Japan, which achieved phenomenal economic development essentially through hard work and frugality and by engaging in trade on its own terms. Japan knew what to learn from others. The decisive question at this point is whether Japan wants other countries to learn from its experience or to be submissive to and dependent on it. I hope the Japanese will tell the world their history – except for the 50 years of militarism and warfare (1894/5–1945), without which the country could have grown even more – and urge others to profit by their example.

IKEDA: It is true that little progress is being made in implementing decisions taken at the 1992 United Nations Conference on the Environment and Development. Of course, dealing with problems of such immense scope is difficult. Even the European Union, which has been enthusiastic about environmental policies, is said to be having trouble in introducing a carbon tax because of distrust

among nations. Even when things are undertaken for the good of
the whole planet, national interests inevitably emerge at the state
level.

You suggest the possibility of a mass popular movement exerting
influence on governmental policies. Surely nongovernmental organizations have a crucial role to play at that level.

It is no longer permissible for the affluent nations of the North
to enjoy a prosperity dependent on sacrifices on the part of the poor
nations of the South. Global society has no tomorrow unless North
and South can achieve harmonious coexistence and shared
prosperity. At no other time in history has it been as essential as it
is now for peoples everywhere to realize this.

Mere day-to-day survival is the concern of the peoples of the less
affluent nations of the world, who are faced with immense difficulties. For instance, when they fell trees for fuel, as they often must,
they destroy resources, damage the environment and contribute
to desertification. Peoples of the richer nations must take these dire
necessities into consideration when they evolve environmental and
economic proposals. I should like to think that Japan could be a
model for other nations in this connection.

We can no longer afford to spend money on the military –
especially in a time of worldwide economic recession. Instead,
basing our thinking and acting on the needs of life, we must
cultivate diverse, self-reliant economies in all parts of the globe.

GALTUNG: Economies must relate equitably. There is nothing
wrong with trade, as long as it is conducted in the right way. It can
be a marvelous instrument of mutual aid. Usually, however, side
effects known as negative externalities are in fact massive structural
violence in the form of exploitation. The exchange between trading
partners must consist of equally challenging undertakings instead
of sophisticated goods being exchanged by one side in return for
raw materials from the other. Both parties must cooperate to
reduce such negative externalities as pollution/depletion.

As I try to indicate in my *Economics in Another Key*, we badly need
a new trade doctrine. The Koran, unlike the Bible, was and is partly
a doctrine of decent, honest trade. But it must be updated to suit
modern conditions. Maybe Mahayana Buddhism could take the
lead here.

IKEDA: Its eagerness for isolation from the rest of the world made
it difficult for Hinayana Buddhism even to think in terms of
Buddhist economics. But the Buddhism of Nichiren Daishonin,
in which we believe, states: 'All the world's governance and industry
is in keeping with the ultimate truth.' As Nichiren Buddhists,
therefore, we are deeply interested in economic affairs and believe

that, at a profound level, Buddhist ideals are connected with all phenomena.

I agree that commercial and trade transactions must be honest. We grow increasingly dependent on each other and on all things. Under such circumstances, instead of concerning ourselves with the prosperity of a single enterprise or a single nation, we must realize that we live in an age demanding symbiosis and prosperity achieved through cooperation. This idea is indispensable to honest trade.

The Buddhist concept of symbiosis, or causal origination, is founded not on individuality but on relationships and mutual dependence. Since all things originate from causation, the phenomenal world is formed on the basis of relationships. In other words, human beings, nonhuman nature, economics and all living things work in mutual interrelationship to create one living world.

On the basis of this idea, Mahayana Buddhism teaches an independent way of life that transcends narrow egoism. This teaching has much to offer in connection with the new rules for honest commerce and morally fair transactions that you highlight.

Armament of the Apocalypse

IKEDA: Although the end of the Cold War has drastically reduced the danger that superpowers will use them, nuclear arms still exist. A single mistake on the part of controllers in any of the nuclear nations of the former Soviet Union could lead to weapons being hijacked. Furthermore, the likelihood that former Soviet nuclear scientists will seek employment in nations eager to expand their own arsenals poses a very real problem.

Because of their immense destructive powers, nuclear weapons must never be thought of within the framework applicable to conventional weapons. In his book *Janus*, Arthur Koestler wrote, 'Since the day when the first atomic bomb outshone the sun over Hiroshima, mankind as a whole has had to live with the prospect of its extinction as a species.'

Centralization of authority in the national state means that modern warfare inevitably involves the concentration of a nation's entire might. Since nuclear weapons were created within the structure of modern technology, the threat they represent can be thought of as an inescapable, potentially catastrophic result of modern civilizational development.

My mentor, Josei Toda, second president of Soka Gakkai, called nuclear weapons Satanic and urged members of peace movements all over the world to strive for their elimination. Carrying out his injunction has been and remains one of my main tasks in life.

GALTUNG: The title chosen for this section is very appropriate. The semitic male deities Jahveh, God and Allah have both the power of genesis and the power of the kind of total destruction foreseen in the apocalypse of the Book of Revelation. In Hinduism, God appears as creator, destroyer and preserver. The semitic deity is wanting in this last attribute. God's self-appointed representatives on Earth were not minor monarchs, but emperors. And modern superpowers have succeeded to the emperors' position. Hence it is only to be expected that they possess instruments of utter destruction, since, in their eyes at least, such arms underlie their godlike character.

Though they may be willing to accept reductions and substitutions, none of the current nuclear nations – the United States, Britain, France, China, India, Russia, Belarus, Ukraine, Kazakhstan, Israel and possibly more – is likely to give up its nuclear arsenal. To do so would mean descending from a superior position. Indeed, other nations want to join the nuclear club because possession of nuclear arms seems to confer a sense of superiority. In addition, free-floating technology from the former Soviet Union may, as you say, be available to them. Even if it is not, they probably will soon develop their own technology. It is not all that difficult. The major motivation for having such weapons is not to use them, but that they confer prestige as a membership card for the nuclear club, as a bargaining chip (megaton explosion against megaton debt) and so on. We can only hope that greater proliferation will make membership of that nuclear club seem shoddy and less attractive.

Josei Toda saw the truth from the very beginning. And his and your attitude toward nuclear arms lends credibility to Soka Gakkai as a peace movement. I only wish more people around the world would express their disgust at the idea that arms of mass destruction symbolize power and status and would tell their leaders that, far from respecting them, they despise nations accumulating such megadeath machines and regard administrators like the nuclear planners of the Cold War as potential mass murderers. By the way, administrators of this kind are still among us, many of them in very high positions.

Political leaders can be expected to reply with the argument that nuclear weapons are to be used only as deterrents. The Cold War actually offered no proof that nuclear weapons deter warfare itself. For one thing, there is no evidence that either party to the conflict ever contemplated an unprovoked attack on the other. Both sides – perhaps especially the Soviet Union – had highly offensive defensive strategies involving the possibility of fighting outside their own country. But after 1982 the Soviet Union adopted a doctrine of not using atomic weapons first in any conflict. Ominously, as of November 1993, the Russia of Boris Yeltsin has returned to the first-strike doctrine.

It can, however, be argued that nuclear weapons proliferation deterred the use of nuclear weapons themselves. Had only one power possessed them, it might well have been tempted to use them. But this is no argument in favor of nuclear arms. Ironically, it might even seem to be a perverse argument in favor of further proliferation. For the sake of mutual deterrence, each nuclear nation might reasonably favor arming all its enemies with nuclear weapons. In the case of a nation like Israel, enemies can be numerous. But surely, instead of encouraging their proliferation as deterrents, it is much more reasonable to outlaw nuclear arms completely. The initiative to achieve this goal by eliciting a pronouncement from the International Court of Justice in The Hague has already advanced considerably.

Perhaps Western nuclear weapons prevented the use of chemical arms in the Gulf War. Even if they did, however, this only means that the effect nuclear weapons have on the possession of conventional methods of mass destruction is similar to the effect they exert on the possession of nuclear weapons. And this in no way means that nuclear possession deters war itself. On the contrary, it may make war more acceptable by changing our general level of tolerance: any war can be accepted as long as it is not a nuclear war. Hitler and Stalin eroded our baseline for tolerating political killing in just this way. By twentieth-century standards, anything less hideous than their crimes has become almost acceptable.

In the light of all these considerations, I urge Soka Gakkai to continue its struggle against these antilife, anticreation devices and their proponents. Though probably not wanted in Washington DC, its exhibition on the effect of nuclear war, shown all over the world, was excellent. People everywhere want more exhibitions demonstrating alternatives.

IKEDA: In all likelihood, a nuclear conflict would be every bit as bloodcurdling and horrible as the Armageddon portrayed in the Book of Revelation. The reign of the Messiah to be established after the Last Judgement and its sufferings represents a universal drama of salvation that has emerged in various forms in most stages of human history. In his analysis of it, the British author D.H. Lawrence (1885–1930) said that, more than a mere projection of hopes for salvation on the part of the oppressed, apocalyptic writing like the Book of Revelation represents the distorted, shadowy desire for revenge against the powerful. He considered its mainstays to be the oppressed's desire to turn the tables on their oppressors. In this sense, you hit the mark when, in slightly different form, you speak of the sense of superiority conferred by possession of nuclear weapons.

Faith in the deterrent effect of nuclear arms casually ignores love and faith and finds support in extremely hypertrophic forms of distrust, fear and hatred. It cannot therefore be called reasonable. It spells the defeat of human nature. Human society must be built on peace, love and trust. Distrust, fear and hatred may sometimes bring more or less brief periods of respite from war, but this is not true peace. Such castles built on sand are doomed to collapse in succeeding periods of conflict. Distrust, fear and hatred rip peoples asunder in a dreadful psychological nuclear fission. The mission of all who are devoted to the cause of peace is to awaken humanity to this truth.

GALTUNG: Like nuclear arms, the ancient Egyptian pyramids were major technological achievements and major displays of power, class and arrogance. It is said that technologies cannot be uninvented. Still, I find the present-day lack of interest in pyramid-building a hopeful sign. Even if they cannot be uninvented, technologies can be phased out. If such were to be the fate of nuclear-arms technology, though the knowledge of their production would persist, no one would care about it. Until it is phased out, however, we must persevere along the path indicated by Toda, Bertrand Russell, Albert Einstein and that marvelous peace organization, International Physicians for the Prevention of Nuclear Warfare, whose nearly 200,000 members in 90 countries all work to make the use of nuclear arms illegitimate.

Proliferation and Supervision of Nuclear Technology

IKEDA: Suspicions about nuclear weapons in such places as Iraq and North Korea threaten the existing nuclear-nonproliferation system. No doubt more and more nations are going to seek ways to dodge stipulations in nonproliferation treaties in order to continue their own nuclear-weapons research and development. This poses one threat to the system. Another is the possibility that nuclear technology and technicians from the former Soviet Union may seek employment in countries that up till now have had no nuclear arsenals.

In addition to minimizing the number of countries capable of producing and stocking such weapons, nonproliferation treaties are intended to limit the expansion of existing nuclear arsenals. This in turn means that, to strengthen the nonproliferation-treaty system, nations must undertake their own nuclear-arms reduction programs.

The tremendous radiation pollution caused by the nuclear accident at Chernobyl in 1986 tragically underscores the threat to all humanity and the importance of international safety and technical-supervision norms for all – peaceful or martial – applications of nuclear energy. Establishing and implementing these norms necessitate the strictest inspections. I have long insisted that the United Nations itself must take the initiative in pioneering a system of nuclear-safety control.

GALTUNG: We should remember that the United States originated nuclear weapons, used them first, has supplied the relevant technology to others and maintains arsenals in several places. Therefore we should not focus solely on the enemies, imagined or real, of the United States but, as you imply, on all countries. The mandate of the International Atomic Energy Agency in Vienna should be strengthened and expanded. Nonetheless, I consider the Indian argument against the current nonproliferation arrangement watertight. India rightly maintains that as long as the five veto-holding members of the United Nations Security Council, who are all nuclear powers by choice as well as the world's five major arms dealers, do not reduce their own nuclear dimensions, the doctrine of nonproliferation only strengthens the present division of the world into states with and states without ultimate power. Nuclear disarmament by these five countries would help enormously. Moreover, the states who now hold Security Council veto powers are not necessarily the same as they were when they were the victors of World War II. The United States and United Kingdom remain the same, but the China and Russia of today are certainly not the Nationalist China and Soviet Union of 1945. And France was hardly a victor anyway. The only things holding these nations together are veto powers: a nuclear veto and a veto on the Security Council. As I have said, it is scarcely strange that other countries should see possession of weapons as a kind of ticket to the acquisition of permanent veto power.

As you say, adequate safeguards against the effects of nuclear experimentation on the ordinary population are of the most pressing importance. The victims of the Chernobyl disaster suffer from a condition known as Chernobyl AIDS: destruction of the immune system as a result of exposure to radiation. This later emerges as high susceptibility to cancer and to colds that develop into pneumonia. With the passing of time, Hiroshima victims, too, have shown similar symptoms. Is it possible that open uranium mining in the former Belgian Congo (Zaïre) or atomic testing near the Equator triggered AIDS and that HIV is only a transmission mechanism? I do not know, but these possibilities indicate the depth of the problem and the complexity of causal chains or cycles.

IKEDA: We must realize fully that, although the Cold War has drawn to a close, the problem of nuclear weaponry persists. The Soviet Union has fallen, and the United States and Russia are in the process of reducing their nuclear arsenals. Nonetheless, optimism is unwarranted. Many questions remain unanswered. How is suitable control to be set up over nuclear weapons in the possession of Ukraine, Belarus and Kazakhstan? Who is to bear the costs of dismantling? What can be done should some fanatic national leader amass a nuclear arsenal? Weapons aside, the safety of nuclear reactors in the former Soviet Union remains in the gravest doubt.

Instead of making the mistake of allowing these issues to drag on into the next century, I hope we will be able to discover promising prospects for their solutions before the present decade is out. A step in the right direction would be for the United States and Russia to halt all nuclear experiments. I cannot condone the development of new small nuclear weapons that the United States is said to be undertaking.

In recent years, the antinuclear peace movements have apparently lost some of their former drive. The time has come to remobilize the power of the people in the name of a perhaps slow, but sure, campaign for dealing with the problem from the standpoint of the belief that nuclear weapons are an absolute evil. Because of the experiences of Hiroshima and Nagasaki, Japan has a major mission in this work.

GALTUNG: I fully agree. But after years of struggling and quarreling between 1945 and 1989, people have somehow grown tired of the nuclear-weapons problem. Perhaps it would be profitable to determine the conditions under which a country or a people would be willing to use nuclear arms. And then we might be able to find out what to do about such circumstances. If underlying conflicts exist, can they be solved in a creative way? I return, therefore, to a vision of Japan's doing the world a favor by serving as a source of creative conflict-transformation going to the roots of the problems of which nuclear arms are symptomatic. But the symptoms, too, demand attention, and right now!

Arms Reduction

IKEDA: Although its ratification remains uncertain, George Bush and Boris Yeltsin did at least sign the second Strategic Arms Reduction Talks (START II in 1992), eliminating all multi-warhead intercontinental ballistic missiles (ICBMs) and restricting the number of strategic-weapons warheads to between 3,000 and 3,500, or about one-third their present levels. Much more drastic reductions would be welcome. Indeed, the total elimination of nuclear weapons from the face of the Earth and the cessation by both nations of all nuclear experimentation are the only acceptable ultimate goal.

GALTUNG: I am afraid that, generally speaking, trying to disarm by destroying arms is rather like trying to cure an alcoholic by destroying every bottle of liquor on Earth. Once all the strong drink is gone, the alcoholic turns to bootlegging. In the case of addiction to arms or addiction to alcohol, the root cause must be found. It is probably not unique to the addict. Remember, many of these countries are arms addicts.

As has been said, in the case of nuclear arms the prestige function is one cause. Possession of nuclear arms makes a power feel like a superpower. It makes Russia and Ukraine, for instance, feel that everything has not yet been lost. In addition, of course, nuclear weapons can be used as bargaining chips for debt reduction. I repeat: megatons for megabucks?

The idea of deterrence is not totally groundless. As has been pointed out, nuclear weapons may have served to deter nations from using nuclear weapons. At present, a triangular formation is taking shape between the European Union, the Russian Union and a possible Turkish Union. In the European Union, the United Kingdom and France are nuclear powers; in the 'Russian Union' there are three such states: Russia, Belarus and Ukraine. Kazakhstan and Pakistan in the ECO probably possess nuclear weapons. Centuries-old conflicts between Catholics and Protestants and between Orthodox Christians, Catholic Christians and Muslims may stimulate desire for deterrence among these powers; moreover distrust may arise from the rapidity with which the European Union integrates, forcing other groups of countries to follow suit. In the future, the world may witness first a race to integrate and then, perhaps, another arms race.

Once again, the best approach to this as to many problems is creative conflict-transformation. Indeed, there is no substitute for it. Arms and arms races are generally more symptomatic than causative. When conflicts exist, big countries amass big arsenals; and small countries usually build up small arsenals. In the absence of conflict, the possession of arms matters little. Obviously then, the conflict must be handled creatively.

To achieve this, pan-European cooperation is a clear possibility. The Conference on Security and Cooperation in Europe (CSCE) has already proved itself useful in terms of political and military cooperation and constitutes a major condition for the conclusion of the final act of the Helsinki Accords of 1975, which contributed to the end of the Cold War. Cooperation among all its 53 members – Protestant, Catholic, Orthodox and Muslim – would be highly productive in the cause of peace.

By now a venerable organization with a fine reputation, the Council of Europe in Strasbourg could also serve as a major setting for cultural and human-rights cooperation, exchanges among young people, the establishment of twinning relations between cities and so on. The pan-European framework established under the Economic Commission for Europe in Geneva could help with economic and ecological cooperation. Such weightier organizations include the Organization for Economic Cooperation and Development (OECD) in Paris, and possibly in the future an extension of the free trade area linking the European Union and the European Free Trade Association (EFTA) and establishing links from the Atlantic to the Pacific. In spite of these already tried and available organizations, however, the supernationalism now gripping Europe – Protestant-Catholic in the west, Orthodox in the northeast, and Muslim in the southeast – makes alignments along the lines of the European Union, the Russian Union and the ECO more likely. In my view, this would be disastrous because it would further activate fault-lines made dramatically visible by the Yugoslav explosion.

IKEDA: I agree on the importance of locating the root cause of the problem and believe that this can be accomplished only by delving into the inner life of humanity. As I have already noted, in 1957 Josei Toda issued his declaration of prohibition on the use of atomic and hydrogen weapons, which he characterized as monstrous, demonic, Satanic, a means of depriving humanity of the very right to life. Ahead of his time, he fundamentally refuted doctrines about the prestige function of these weapons and all attempts to justify their possession.

Now that the Soviet Union and the United States no longer confront each other with horrendous arsenals, not even their supposed deterrence value justifies the maintaining of any nuclear weapons at all – let alone thousands of them. And this is true in the face of all the demands of the military-industrial complex.

In connection with what you say about nuclear arms as a deterrence against their own use, I insist that we must approach this issue, too, from the standpoint of worldwide nuclear disarmament and the cessation of nuclear-weapons proliferation. One way to do this may be to link aid with halting nuclear proliferation. For example, the Western industrialized nations agreed to increase economic aid to South Africa when it accepted a treaty preventing nuclear proliferation in 1991.

Of course you are entirely correct in saying that the best disarmament policy is to eliminate conflict. But we must not overlook the seriousness of arms exports. Industrialized Western nations are to be severely censured for exporting the armaments with which conflicting armies kill and maim each other.

Eliminating conflicts requires the creation of regional security structures conceived of on a global scale. Using the CSCE as a reference, we must devise similar bodies to suit the needs of other regions of the world. The task requires perseverance and patience; but I am optimistic because, as the European Union may show, we can put faith in human wisdom.

GALTUNG: Certainly the European Union is an almost classic example of how former enemies, such as France and Germany, can begin cooperating. What they can do together, however, may also become a problem. Even if Germany did play the major role, the European Union's premature recognition of Croatia and Bosnia-Herzegovina in 1992 was a disaster. Furthermore, the recognition came in spite of specific warnings and admonitions from Perez de Cuellar, who was United Nations secretary-general at the time. As this indicates and as we all know too well, human wisdom has its limitations.

Global Government

IKEDA: The existence of nuclear weapons compels humanity to reconsider the nature of war. The scientists who participated in their invention know more about nuclear arms than anyone else. It is therefore significant that, when he heard of the bombing of Hiroshima, Albert Einstein uttered a groan of sorrow. Perhaps recognition of his own responsibility in the tragedy inspired him to become an ardent advocate of the movement to establish a global government. Linus Pauling once told me that Einstein felt he might have been mistaken to sign a letter to President Roosevelt recommending the production of atomic bombs.

Einstein saw that the vastly destructive and murderous scale of nuclear weapons reduced the so-called absolute nature of warring sovereign states to insignificant folly. Unfortunately, however, in his time too few people shared his views. And as the Cold War impasse deepened, it seemed that the greatest physicist of the twentieth century had issued his warnings in vain.

But times have changed. Today, after the appearance of Gorbachev and his emphasis on the interests of humanity above those of national states, Einstein's perspicacity may again receive general recognition.

Einstein did not believe that a world government would necessarily be entirely good. As long as government exists, abuses are likely. Still, with all its faults, a world government is preferable to war, the greatest of all evils. Einstein envisioned world government as an emergency structure necessary to bring about the cessation of warfare.

Today humanity longs for peace. The United Nations both symbolizes this shared longing and serves as an assembly for deliberation among the nations of the world. Strengthening the United Nations seems to be an excellent way of putting Einstein's ideas of world government to good use.

GALTUNG: Many of the physicists who worked on the atomic bomb were Jewish. It must have been a shock for them to learn that the weapon had been used to kill not Germans in Berlin or Hamburg, but Japanese in Hiroshima. Would Einstein have uttered the same groan of sorrow had the reverse been the case? We shall never know.

Personally I fear world governments and prefer the weaker formulation I discuss in Chapter 8, 'World Central Governance', in my book of 1980, *The True Worlds*, based on soft power, as envisioned by the Commission on Global Governance, too. As I spell out my reasons for this attitude, I shall point out some of the abuses you say are likely.

A central government has four tasks: cultural integration, economic coordination, the use of violence to control internal and external enemies, and political decision-making in connection with the other three tasks.

Today, cultural integration would be based on Western culture, with all its strengths and weaknesses. A world coordination weaker than a government's, however, would amount to a confederation of cultures. Still, if the world is to be managed as a federation – to say nothing of a unitary nation – solid cultural integration based probably on the English language, Western science and technology, Western human rights and, above all, Western power-arrogance would be necessary.

Should such a federation ever come into being, Western power-arrogance would have arrived precisely where it has always wanted to be: in the very center of the whole world. Nothing less. The missionary command issued in Matthew XXVIII: 19 will have been executed in its secular variety: 'Go ye therefore, and make disciples of all the nations, baptizing them in the name of the Father, and of the Son, and of the Holy Ghost.' The result could be a tremendous loss of world cultural diversity, which is already down from about 4,000 cultures 500 years ago to about 1,000 now.

Economically, a world government could mean world planning and a global marketplace – something similar to what, in spite of all liberal-conservative ideology, exists in the United States now and is referred to as 'managed trade'. I am afraid that these inevitabilities would give birth to a government machinery which would make the Soviet Union seem modest by comparison. For one thing, 20 times more people would be involved. Some people might say the economy could be left to market forces. But I suspect that, once a world government came into existence, people would be unwilling to accept market-force brutality. I envisage the military, which would then be referred to as 'world police', engaged in an endless series of Gulf wars and Somalias conducted with the same savagery and self-righteousness and fully supported by a representative parliament in the name of all humanity, of the whole world.

Perhaps decision-making in a world government can be democratic and express majority will. But I worry about the fate of the inevitably numerous minorities. With his dangerous and seductive formula, the English philosopher and writer Jeremy Bentham (1748–1832) spoke of the greatest happiness for the greatest number of persons, and in doing so laid the foundation for a majoritarian dictatorship in which economic wealth is measured on the basis of gross national product. In contrast to the Benthamite system, Gandhi spoke of fulfilling the basic needs of the least among us and of achieving consensus democracy, even though it is time-consuming. In short, in the case of a world government, I fear we are up against one more rational and very dangerous abstraction, of a kind different, it is true, from the one that brought the Soviet Union into being.

My own vision of an ideal world is looser and more flexible. I think in terms of strong local governments at the small-unit level (village or township), where basic needs are satisfied. These units could then enter into a confederation of countries constituting a world confederation of regions or civilizations.

A federation dictates common financial, foreign and military policies. As the Confederacy of Southern States learned in the United States Civil War, there is no way out of a federation. A confederation is based on coordinated autonomy in financial, foreign and military policy; and the covenant among its members is renegotiable. It provides an escape clause with appropriate warnings and time limits. This corresponds better to the realities of our very complex world and serves the key dimensions of diversity and symbiosis better.

Caution is needed, however, because people in monotheistic cultures tend to favor unicentral political constructions. Confederations are better for polytheists and pluralists. Their strong local bases even give them a pantheistic element. Monotheism invites submission and the anticipation of either praise or punishment from above. Polytheism offers more variety: if one god fails, there is always another to turn to. Pervasive, immanent pantheism links human and nonhuman nature; it is more in harmony with the

Buddhist approach. This alone is a good reason for my intuitive preference for the loose, flexible solution I have indicated.

Viewed from this standpoint, the United Nations begins to look better. Perhaps its very inefficiencies are really blessings in disguise in that they prevent the organization from becoming a United States or, worse, a Soviet Union writ large. Perhaps we should preserve the United Nations as it is, except for trying to make it more United Peoples instead of merely United Nations in nature.

IKEDA: I agree that the optimum global governing system would be a loose one. Cultural integration, the first of the tasks you assign to a world government, would be unacceptable if it reduced cultural diversity by means of standardization. Interestingly, the post-modernist movement gropes for diversity of identity to replace the universalist monotony of modernism. You and I agree that any attempts to standardize this movement forcibly would be not only contrary to the times, but also doomed to failure.

Jean-Jacques Rousseau (1712–78) and Immanuel Kant (1724–1804) thought long and hard – mainly on the political level – about the concept of a world system transcending the sovereign-state framework. Both warned against standardization. Rousseau thought always in terms of the extent to which the rights of union could be expanded without infringing on sovereignty. Kant limited the purpose of interstate union to the maintenance of peace. He insisted that union among states intended only to prevent war was the one legal condition consonant with the liberty of the states. Both philosophers pointed out the danger of a hypertrophic world system as a power structure.

I have always insisted that free initiative must be taken into consideration in the creation of any world-integration system. Free initiative must not be violated, even should the issue of limitations on the rights of sovereign states – a topic currently in the international spotlight – be in danger of infringement. To do so would be to sacrifice the important in the name of the less significant or, as the Japanese proverb has it, 'To straighten the horn and kill the cow'.

Any government that deprives its members of free initiative is certain to evolve into a power structure even more monstrous than the Soviet Union. Avoiding this requires respect for the will of the people and the ability to draw on and reflect that will. It is in this connection that I see the greatest importance of your idea of a union not of states, but of peoples. I, too, have frequently proposed making the United Nations an organization in which humanity, not nation states, are most conspicuous. In the years to come, non-governmental organizations should have a big part to play in bringing about the desired conversion.

GALTUNG: The answer is dialogue, inner and outer, among all parties concerned. Crowded on this Earth, we find that our karmas all intersect. When something goes wrong, we should follow the excellent Buddhist tradition of meditating within ourselves and seeking solutions among ourselves. In addition, we must project the Buddhist idea that, far from being a gift from above, self-improvement, individual and collective, while possible, results only from hard work.

The work for peace needs not merely a handful of governments or peoples at the top, but all of us. I am very much afraid that a world government might become a God-substitute, omnipresent, omniscient and omnipotent, of whose benevolence I am by no means sure. Ultimately, we can rely on ourselves and, as you say, on the eternal – the wheel of life which lies beyond our finitude as individuals.

Bibliography of Works Cited

Works by Johan Galtung

Buddhism: A Quest for Unity and Peace (Honululu: Dae Won Sa Pagoda, 1988. Colombo: Sarvodaya, 1993).

Economics in Another Key (forthcoming).

Education for Peace and Development (forthcoming).

Human Rights in Another Key (Cambridge: Polity Press, 1984).

Japan in the World Community: Eight Lectures in Peace Research (English edition forthcoming).

Methodology and Development (Copenhagen: Ejlers, 1988).

'A Structural Theory of Imperialism', ch. 13 in *Essays in Peace Research* (Copenhagen: Ejlers, 1980).

Theories and Methods of Social Research (New York: Columbia University Press, 1967).

There are Alternatives! (Nottingham: Spokesman, 1984).

The True Worlds (New York: Macmillan/Free Press, 1980).

United Nations; United Peoples (forthcoming).

USA Glasnost, with Richard Vincent (forthcoming).

'1989 Fall in East Europe: What Happened and Why?', in *Research in Social Movements* (Greenwich CT: JAI, 1992).

Works by Daisaku Ikeda

The Human Revolution 5 vols (New York and Tokyo: John Weatherhill, 1972–84).

A Lifelong Quest for Peace, with Linus Pauling (Boston, MA: Jones and Bartlett, 1992).

Works by Other Authors

Nini Roll Anker, *Woman and the Black Bird* (Oslo: Aschehoug, 1945).

Confucian *Analects* (London: Allen and Unwin, 1938).

Confucius, *Way of Humanity*.

Jacques Duroselle, *L'Europe: Histoire de ses peuples* (Gütersloh: Perrin and Bertelsmann, 1990).

Johan Perter Eckersmann, *Gespräche mit Goethe in den letzten Jahren seines Lebens* (Wiesbaden: Insel Verlag, 1955).

Foreign Press Center Japan, *Japan and the World in the Post-Cold War Era* (Tokyo: Foreign Press Center, 1990).

Francis Fukuyama, 'The End of History?', in *National Interest*, 1989.

Yukichi Fukuzawa, *Bunmei-ron no Gairyaku*.

Mahatma Gandhi, *All Men Are Brothers* (New York: Continuum, 1990).

Boutros Boutros-Ghali, *An Agenda for Peace* (New York: United Nations, 1992).

Goethe, *Faust*.

Vaclav Havel, *Disturbing the Peace: A Conversation with Karel Hvizdala* (New York: Knopf, 1990).

Eduard Heimann, *Soziale Theorie der Wirtschaftssyteme* (Tübingen: J.C.B. Mohr, 1963).

William James, *The Moral Equivalent of War* (Rutland, Vermont: C.E. Tuttle, 1969).

Ichiro Kawasaki, *Japan Unmasked* (Rutland, Vermont: C.E. Tuttle, 1969).

Arthur Koestler, *Janus: A Summing Up* (New York: Random House, 1978)

Arthur Koestler *et al*, *The God That Failed* (New York: Harper, 1950).

V.I. Lenin, *The State and Revolution* (London: Lawrence and Wishart, 1969).

Karl Marx and Frederick Engels, *The Communist Manifesto* (Harmondsworth: Penguin Books, 1967)

Mojing

Michel de Montaigne, *Essais* (Paris: Librairie Générale Française, 1972).

Nagarjuna, *Mula-madyamaka-shastra*.

Nichiren Shoshu International Center, *A Dictionary of Buddhist Terms and Concepts* (Tokyo: Nichiren Shoshu International Center, 1983).

Arthur M. Schlesinger Jr, *The Disunity of America: Reflections on a Multicultural Society* (New York: W. W. Norton, 1992).

Ernst Schumacher, *Small is Beautiful: A Study of Economics as if People Mattered* (New York: Muller, Blond and White, 1973).

P.A. Sorokin, *Social and Cultural Dynamics* (Boston, MA: Porter Sargent, 1956).

South Commission, *The Challenge of the South* (Oxford: Oxford University Press, 1990).

Alvin Toffler, *Powershift: Knowledge, Wealth and Violence at the Edge of the 21st Century* (New York: Bantam Books, 1990).

Leon Vandermeersch, *le Nouveau monde sinise* (Paris: Presses Universitaires de France, 1986).

Voltaire, *Traité sur la tolérance* (Geneva, 1763).

World Commission on Environment and Development, *Our Common Future* (Oxford: Oxford University Press, 1987).

Index

abortion 79
abstractions, are not absolutes 100–1
activism, Gandhi's 57
aggression, sublimation of 68–71
AIDS 153
Aitmatov, Chingiz 18, 44
Alain, Émile-August Chartier 20
American War of Independence 63, 109
anger, Buddhist state of 70–1
Anker, Nini Roll 10
Arab nationalism 120, 121, *see also* Islam
Ariès, Philippe 15
arms trade 157, *see also* nuclear weapons
art, power of 11–12
Asia, Japan's role in 141–2

belligerence, sublimation of 68–71
Bentham, Jeremy 159
Bergson, Henri 39–40, 88
black movements, peaceful 58
Bodhisattva state of Buddhism 70, 71, 74, 77
boundaries, removal of 74
Boutros-Ghali, Boutros 133, 140
British Empire 58, 59
Brundtland, Gro Harlem, chair of UNCED 25
Brzezinski, Zbigniew 45, 46, 47

Buddhism x–xi, 75, 80, 95, 111; Buddha Law and society 83; Buddha nature 94–5; Eightfold Path 85, 87; Five Precepts 90, 92; Four Evil Paths 70–1, 74; Four Noble Truths 85, 86–7; Four Noble Worlds 74; Four Sufferings 6; limitations of 78, 79–88; Nine Consciousnesses 72–3; Ten States of Life 70, 71, 122–3; Three Evil Paths 70; Three Realms of Existence 74; Three Virtues 87; transmigration of life energy (karma) 72–5, *see also* Hinayana; Mahayana; Shakyamuni

capitalism: expansionism of 53–4; failings of 45, 46, 47; in former communist countries 47, 49–50; of periphery 116
Cassin, René 109–10
caste system, Gandhi's view of 65, 66
causal origination 92–5, 149
censorship, by taboo 42–3
challenges, accepting 3–5
Chernobyl disaster 152–3
children: education of 15–16; influence of family on 23–4
China 117
Christianity 75, 76–7; intolerance of 78; soft 102, *see also* Roman Catholicism

Index by Auriol Griffith-Jones